FIRMLY PLANTED PUBLICATIONS

An imprint of Equipped for Life Ministries, Dallas, Texas

# The Road to Heaven?

## Constructed by Men Alone

## A Response to

## *Not All Roads Lead to Heaven*

### B. Dale Taliaferro

*Road to Heaven?*
*Constructed by Men Alone*
Published by Firmly Planted Publications
An imprint of Equipped for Life Ministries

Copyright © 2018 by B. Dale Taliaferro
International Standard Book Number:
978-1-950072-02-6

Printed copies sold at Logos Book Store, 6620 Snider Plaza, Dallas, Texas, 75205-3483

Scripture quotations taken from the New American Standard Bible®, Copyright © 1960, 1962, 1963, 1968, 1971, 1972, 1973, 1975, 1977, 1995 by The Lockman Foundation (www.Lockman.org). Used by permission.

For information:
Equipped for Life Ministries
P.O. Box 12013
Dallas, Texas 75225
U.S.A.

Library of Congress Number:

First Edition / First Printing / 2018

## A Shrinking World Requires a Better Christianity

Then a direct comparison is made between what has been accepted as orthodox Christianity and what the Bible *explicitly* says about salvation. This book is a rebuttal of Robert Jeffress' book, *NOT all roads LEAD to HEAVEN*, and is entitled:

## Living through Crises

This book illustrates the extraordinary life that Jesus gives to all who believe Him for it.

## Living through Crises Leader's Guide

Through a series of questions with the answers given, the reader is taught to personalize the principles in the main book.

## Living through Crises Study Guide

This book offers some of the questions that are covered in the Leader's Guide for the student to fill in before discussing them in the small group.

## Judas and Divine Grace, revised edition

The proofs are given herein that Judas had believed in Jesus, had received eternal life, had followed Jesus faithfully, and will be in the coming Kingdom of Messiah.

# The Contents

# Preface

One morning after my Thursday morning Bible study Jim came into my office and said, "I think you should write a response to this book." The book to which Jim was referring was written by Robert Jeffress, and is entitled *Not All Roads Lead to Heaven.*[1]

After some discussion with Jim on the matter I said that I would read it and then decide. After reading it, I felt that it was an outstanding example of traditional, Christian orthodoxy. In addition, it was written simply and very clearly. Moreover, it dealt with most of the classic verses that orthodox Christianity uses to support its position before the world. And when the persons recommending the book are taken into account, it would be hard to debate the fact that the message presented in the book reflects mainline, evangelical thinking.

Consequently, I told Jim the following week that I would write a response to the ideas presented in the book and to the exegesis used to support those ideas. After writing my response, I passed it on to others for their critique. The manner in which this presentation comes is the result of many eyes analyzing both the material and the tone taken in this response. It is the hope of all of us that the tone will be acceptable to the reader to encourage him to engage objectively with the material being presented.

I want to make it crystal clear at the very beginning that this presentation is not an attack on the author of the book that is being used to guide our discussion. A plethora of other books

---

[1] All references to this book and to the Christian theology that it represents, the same theology that I too was taught in seminary, from this point forward will be made using the abbreviation NAR (for Not All Roads ...).

devoted to the topic of salvation could have been used. This book was chosen because it is a very clear and admirably simple presentation of the common belief found throughout evangelical Christendom today. My Bible studies are on a journey of verification and discovery: we are trying to verify what we've been taught and in the process discover what the Bible actually says rather than what various theologies have tried to convince us that it says. Any attempt to systematize the ideas or overall message of the Bible is susceptible to the supposition that certain concepts are the same when in fact they are quite different. These differences must be discovered and their impact must be recognized.

Like the author of NAR, I too was taught the exact perspective on salvation that he presents in his book. About fourteen years ago I would not have had an issue with anything in NAR. But now I find that many of the verses that have been used to support the doctrines that we both have been taught have been taken out of their contexts, isolated, and made to support preconceived (i.e., theological) ideas.

But like the author of NAR, I too believe that the Bible is the Word of God. I too believe that it is inerrant and infallible though it can be badly misinterpreted. I too believe that the Bible should be taken literally, even understanding that figures of speech have a literal and specific meaning. Whatever the Bible teaches is to be accepted as God's perspective on the topic under discussion.

I too have studied the Bible for decades. Almost five to be exact. I continue to have a ministry that reaches to distant lands, training other Christian leaders in the message of the Bible and in the proper method for interpreting the Bible. I received my training in this discipline (which is generally referred to as Hermeneutics) from Dr. Earl Radmacher, who was the president and a professor of systematic theology at Western Seminary, Portland, Oregon. His abridged book on Hermeneutics, the discipline of interpreting the Scriptures, can still be obtained through The Timothy Initiative Publications in West Palm Beach, Florida. The power to critique what you are reading or what you are hearing someone advocate makes you less vulnerable to being led astray by innocent sounding ideas which are really unbiblical.

When I finally began to use my seminary training in hermeneutics to critique what I had been taught, I was surprised at what I discovered. Some of those discoveries will be laid before you in the course of responding to the traditional expositions promoted by NAR and used to defend the doctrine of salvation handed down to us by the Reformers. I believe you will be surprised as I was at those conclusions.

I sincerely hope this book causes a renewed discussion on the doctrine of salvation with the intent of discovering what the Bible *explicitly* says about each topic covered herein. If it only causes us to retreat back to our theological reference books, we will only prolong the spiritual defeat and heartache of the sheep that God has allotted to us.

One caveat that should be mentioned in the beginning concerns the reference that I make in this book to orthodox Christian beliefs. That reference does not include every variation of orthodoxy within Christendom. It only refers to one specific stream of theology that can be traced back to a specific time and place, but one that has seemingly permeated and dominated much of the religious thought in western Christianity. This theology which the author of NAR shares in his treatise is the same theological perspective that I was taught. I find it necessary now to reconsider it objectively, a task I was unable to do when I was first taught it.

But much of what is said here applies equally to the other versions of Christian orthodoxy as well since all versions have basically the same concepts of justification, salvation, eternal life, forgiveness, and the kingdom of heaven as do those who are still passing down to us the theology of the Reformation. Their attempts to systematize these concepts have blurred the individual distinctiveness of each of these terms. It will be our job to bring them back into proper focus. After all, don't we all want to believe what God has revealed, and that alone?

# Introduction

A great many Christians have questions about the faith that has been taught to them. The longer that we all live and the more exposure we have to the rest of the world, the more questions keep arising. For example,

Have you ever wondered about your own salvation?

Have you wondered about those within the Christian faith that don't believe exactly like you do?

Have you ever wondered about the effectiveness of death bed conversions?

Have you ever wondered about the destiny of those who have never had the privilege of hearing the message about Jesus?

Have you ever wondered about the eternal destiny of some of those of other faiths who have as good a character as many of the Christians that you know?

We all have these questions so don't think that there is something wrong with you or your faith because you have them. These kinds of questions lead us to examine our faith to confirm how closely it represents the truth *explicitly* taught in the Bible.

Hans Christian Andersen wrote a short tale entitled "The Emperor's New Clothes."[1] Actually the emperor had no clothes on at all, but everyone was afraid to say so! Finally, a very young, naïve lad blurted out the obvious truth that many others recognized but were restrained for various reasons from declaring what they suspected to be true. As I tell the story, I hope you will readily

---

[1] This little introduction to Andersen's short story was taken from an article I wrote for my blog entitled "Forgiveness, Everyone wants it, but for the wrong reason!" The blog is called Maverick-Ministers.com. Andersen first published *The Emperor's New Clothes*, a Danish fairy tale, in 1837.

understand the application I'm making of it to the soteriology (the doctrine of salvation) that has been accepted as the official position of evangelical Christianity for over five hundred years.

It goes like this: There once lived a king who cared excessively about fine clothes. He loved to show them off whenever he could. One day he heard from two men who were swindlers in disguise. They claimed that they could make the finest suit of clothes from the most beautiful cloth ever seen. This cloth, they said, also had a special quality about it: *it was invisible to anyone who was either stupid or unfit for his position.*

It occurred to the king that he himself might not be able to see the cloth. And if he couldn't see it, he would be declaring to all of his subjects that he was unfit to be king. So the king first sent two of his most loyal and trusted men to see it. Of course, neither of them wanted to admit that he could not see the cloth. That would be an admission that they were either stupid or unfit to be the king's royal servants. So, they both naturally praised it.

All of the townspeople by this time had also heard of this amazing cloth and were interested in discovering how stupid their neighbors were. They were not concerned about themselves of course. (Their response seems wildly similar to all of the "spiritual fruit-checkers" today. But I digress.) They knew they were fine even when they were compared to people who had better character and lifestyles than they had. Somehow they knew that their flaws were not serious enough to omit them from the ranks of the acceptable.

The king then allowed himself to be dressed in these extraordinary clothes for a procession through town. He never admitted that he too could not see the cloth. Not wanting to be seen as stupid or unfit for the throne, he went along with the swindlers' charade. After all, did he not have the explicit support of those closest to him and the implicit support of all of his subjects?

Of course, all the king's subjects wildly praised the magnificent clothes, being too embarrassed to admit that they could not see them.

Finally, during the procession through town a small child said: "But he has nothing on!"

The child's innocent observation was whispered from person to person until everyone in the crowd was shouting that the emperor had nothing on. The king, of course, heard the shouts and now intuitively knew that they were true. But admitting to the deception would reveal his own stupidity and unfitness to rule his kingdom so he held his head high and finished the royal procession.

The expressions "the Emperor's new clothes" and "the Emperor has no clothes" are often used to refer to a situation in which *the majority of observers willingly maintain a collective ignorance about facts that are all too obvious to the objective observer.* And even many in this majority might individually recognize the absurdity of the position being promoted, but out of fear for losing their standing among the rest, they keep silent.

Others have emphasized another point of Andersen's tale: the idea that *truth is often spoken by a person too naïve or too inexperienced to understand the power of group pressures within a given sub-culture.* Until the sub-culture trains him not to do so, he might hold convictions that are contrary to the beliefs of all those around him because those conclusions initially seem so obvious to him. But with further training from the culture around him, he begins to see everything the way everyone else around him sees them. His personal convictions are silenced and eventually overturned by the convictions of the majority. He becomes one of the many.

In religious matters, some have called this *consensus theology*. That phrase simply observes that the conclusions drawn by some who have distinguished themselves (either by their intellect, or their leadership, or in any number of other ways) are usually handed down without much debate from generation to generation. The conclusions themselves are no longer open to questioning; they must be followed. It is assumed that no better answer can be given. As a result, the vast majority accepts those conclusions and passes them down to future generations as the accepted and unquestioned position of the Christian faith.

I believe that Christian theologians have followed and have passed down to the church in general a very *rational perspective* of the message of the Bible. But that message, as it turns out, is badly flawed. A perspective can be *extremely logical* and yet not be, at the same time, true to the facts that exist.

This is, of course, how individuals in the past have been convicted of crimes that they didn't commit. The arguments against them were logical and convincing but, at the same time, dismissive of other facts that seemed to point in the opposite direction. Sometimes these additional facts weren't even presented or known at the time of the original examination so that the judgment or sentencing was given without their influence or impact. When they were finally brought forward later, they changed the whole balance of evidence and overturned the previous way of thinking completely. Consequently, the judgment had to be reversed. A better decision had now come to light.

This is what I believe has happened in the development of the Christian doctrine on salvation. Changes have been introduced so thoughtfully that almost everyone, who was not spending the time and the enormous amount of effort to test the foundation of what was being taught, has become quite comfortable with *errant truth* or *heretical orthodoxy* if you will. It is *truth* in the sense that it has been accepted as orthodox for over five hundred years. But it is still *errant* because it is incorrect, having no *explicit* Scriptural foundation.

The level of comfort that exists among Christians with doctrines that cannot be found *explicitly* stated in the Bible is alarming. A defensive wall automatically rises whenever a person challenges what has become acceptable or what is perceived to be the unquestionable truth of Christianity.

I was completely comfortable with the tenets that I had been taught, thinking that there was no better presentation of the subject matter possible. I also experienced this defensiveness each time someone had the audacity to question what I believed to be true. Since our eternal destiny *supposedly* rides on understanding the doctrine of salvation correctly, this is no small or insignificant matter.

I will work hard to keep the discussion simple and clear. The author of NAR did a marvelous job of presenting the discussion that way in his book. I only hope I can do as well in this response to his presentation. The basic issue of disagreement that I have with the classic Christian perspective that NAR outlines for us is this: *Salvation is simply and definitively not about going to heaven.* The belief of classic Christianity that there is a road to heaven, and that it can be gained only through faith in Jesus, to use Andersen's fairy tale, constitutes the clothes that can't be seen (verified) without major, Biblically unsupportable assumptions being used. Since few are willing to step forward and declare the obvious because no one wants to be viewed as stupid or unfit for further

Christian service, I have done this with the hope of leading the discussion back to what the Bible actually says. Those willing to test what they believe by the *explicit* teachings of the Bible have made this a wonderfully fun and joyous experience. But unfortunately not all are open to question what they have been taught.

The backlash from Christian Bible colleges, from seminaries, from leaders who have taught that salvation was about getting to heaven must be expected. But to hold onto that theory of salvation, a person has to make one *assumption* after the other. It is my conviction, formed after fourteen years of study on this topic, that none of these *assumptions* have the slightest bit of *explicit* support from the Scriptures when they are properly interpreted by following sound hermeneutical principles.

Not all errors are equally devastating just like not all losses in football are equally devastating. A loss in the SEC championship game is not the same as a loss during the regular season. The ultimate goal of a national championship can still be in reach after a regular season loss. But a loss in the SEC championship game usually means that the national championship has slipped away. A loss in that game prevents the ultimate goal from being reached.

In the same way the discovery of an error in *assumptive* or *conjectural* material is a loss only to the unyielding traditionalist. To all the rest such a discovery is a win, making the whole more sound than before. In this latter case, the goal is still reachable, in this life, in the coming age, and in the age after that when God creates a new heaven and a new earth.

When NAR suggests that "the single greatest stumbling block for nonbelievers coming to faith in Christ is the issue of [Christianity's claim to] exclusivity" on page fourteen, it is only saying what Christianity has said for hundreds of years. And with this conclusion, I tend to agree. Christianity's claim to be the exclusive way to heaven is a tremendous hindrance to others coming to faith in Jesus. In fact, that is the reason this book is being written. *Christianity has been, and still is, turning people away at the door based upon a Biblically unsupportable doctrine.*

When Christianity makes a claim to exclusiveness, it is referring to its teaching that faith in Jesus is *the only way for a person to get to heaven.*[1] This is, for classic Christianity, an essential doctrine. Consequently, the question that NAR seeks to answer is, "Don't all religions lead to heaven?" The only answer that Christianity accepts for that question is simply stated in this way:

> "Not all roads lead to heaven – only the road through saving faith in Jesus Christ does."[2]

*Unproven assumptions* fill the pages of the book we are trying to critique because *unproven assumptions* are used to support the belief that heaven is reached by faith in Jesus alone. We certainly want to win each person with whom we dialogue to faith in Jesus. But the purpose of such belief is not to obtain a ticket to heaven. The purpose is far, far greater than that! We will cover that purpose as we proceed in our study of the supposed doctrine of exclusivity to which Christianity clings.

---

[1] NAR, p. 15.
[2] Ibid.

# Chapter 1

# Surveying the Four Suggested Roads to Heaven

Generally speaking, there are four popular answers to the question, "Who will be in heaven?" Those answers reflect the four most dominate worldviews today according to NAR. They are universalism, pluralism, inclusivism, and exclusivism (this last view is, of course, that of orthodox Christianity which was finally formulated in many of its present aspects by the Reformers of the sixteenth and seventeenth centuries). These four worldviews become the theological "labels" that we place on those who differ with us.

But all labeling has disadvantages as well as advantages. First, does the label properly describe the person it is meant to describe? Does the label, that might have been used in the past, still adequately describe a person today? Apparently, labels change as each culture changes so that they can be somewhat different today or at least somewhat more subjective.

A person might describe himself as a mixture of universalism and inclusivism. But to come away from those labels with only very general ideas as to what they mean is to place a label upon him and force him into a descriptive category that doesn't really fit his full beliefs on the matters in question.

Mislabeling someone is similar to the use of guilt by association. In the matters before us in this presentation, guilt should not be levied upon anyone until it has been proven that he misunderstands the Scriptures that he should be following.

After recently talking to my tenth grade Spanish teacher, I

found out that I had been labeled back in high school. I had taken a Spanish language aptitude test, which I have no recollection of doing. She told me that according to all the experts who developed the test, I would never be able to learn Spanish and probably any other language either. As we were getting caught up, she told me what she had been doing over all these years, and I told her about my doctorate. To pursue my doctorate I had classes to learn to read Biblical Greek and Hebrew and pass reading exams for French and German. All of which I successfully accomplished. My former Spanish teacher then said that not only was she glad to hear this but that I had also proven all the experts wrong (referring to the people who had devised the language aptitude test I had taken in the tenth grade).

My point is to simply say this: labels can be limiting, half correct, or entirely wrong. As a result, we will use these widely used descriptions of the four worldviews only as suggestive guidelines in order to discuss the claim of orthodox Christianity of being the one and only exclusive way to get to heaven.

Don't become distressed, then, by the fact that you don't see yourself completely described in any of these traditional worldviews. That really is not the important thing here, nor is it the reason they are used. NAR's goal is to confirm and defend the suggestion of Christian exclusivism. The other three worldviews are used merely to set up the discussion about the exclusive claims that Jesus *supposedly* made for being the only way for a person to arrive in heaven. Jesus' *supposed* claims to exclusivism are generally called the *grace factor* or the *gospel of grace* in NAR, which gospel formulation so simply and clearly represents the belief of all of Christendom, generally speaking. The escape from hell and the obtainment of heaven are free gifts the book says. All one has to do to get these free gifts, according to NAR, is to believe in Jesus. So, heaven is unattainable to those without faith in Jesus. If you are a Christian, this most likely sounds exactly like what you have been taught, doesn't it? It is what I was taught.

The second problem that the reader faces when he interacts with any kind of labeling is determining whether a fair critique has been given of each view. The four options are typically set forth to describe who will make it to heaven and the reasons that they will get there. From NAR's point of view, if Jesus is the only way to heaven, then none of these other three options can provide a pathway to heaven. Consequently, none of the other three can have any Biblical support relative to that specific goal of getting to heaven after one dies.

But we will find that such is not the case. While NAR uses the other three as little more than strawmen to convince the reader that Jesus is the only real option for obtaining heaven, we will show that all three of these other options have some Biblical support undergirding them. They may need to be redefined here and there, but there are reasons for not rejecting them wholesale.

## Universalism: A Good Expectation for All

Universalism, according to NAR,[1] is generally defined in this way:

"...the belief that everyone, regardless of his or her *belief* or *unbelief*, will be *accepted by God* for all eternity. This view affirms that *all* people will be ultimately *saved* and that *no one will experience God's punishment*."[2] (emphases mine)

---

[1] Remember that NAR is an abbreviation for Robert Jeffress' book, *Not All Roads Lead to Heaven*, presenting classic Christian views on salvation.

[2] NAR, p. 43. It later includes some universalists into another category called inclusivists who, it says, believe that the death of Christ was meant to save the world (p. 44).

How should we evaluate this statement? When one studies the post-death judgments, he finds that the place *where a person ends up in the afterlife has nothing to do with what he believes in this present life*. Did you know that? It is quite the shocking statement if you have never heard it before. But all future judgments are based upon *works* as Dr. John Walvoord has shown in his listing of the seven coming judgments.[1] As a result, a universalist who is trying to follow the Bible may indeed believe in a coming judgment, but his belief system will not be the subject covered in his judgment. This is true for all people, including Christians as 2Cor. 5:10, among several other passages that could be referenced, tells us.

Second, *it is absolutely not true that all people will ultimately be saved*. To be a universalist today one does not need to believe that all people will be saved. The reason is simple. Being saved and going to heaven to be with God or being saved and being with God on the new earth underneath the new heavens (Rev. 21-22) are not equivalents; they are not synonyms.[2] With the recognition of these truths, the belief system of the universalist changes significantly. *Salvation is not about obtaining heaven*. When that fact is received, everything will change.

Now take a look at your favorite verses on salvation. Do they really *explicitly* say what you have been taught to believe about salvation? Or do they need to be *explained* in a way that results in the meaning that you have been taught?

Do your verses *explicitly* say, "You have been (or can be) saved *from hell* if you . . . [do such and such]?" Or do they *explicitly* say "You have been saved *for heaven* because you did …. [such and such}?" If your verses don't say something like this, then you may

---

[1] John F. Walvoord, *The Millennial Kingdom*, pp. 276ff.
[2] For a full discussion on salvation see my book, *The Grand Spiritual Assumption*. Is salvation really about heaven?

not have the support from the Bible that you thought you had relative to the topic of salvation.

> *What if* salvation does not deal with escaping hell?
> *What if* salvation does not deal with going to heaven?
> *What if* salvation is not a state that a person enters, guaranteeing him a certain destiny in the afterlife?
> *What if* salvation is confined to this world alone?[1]

Third, it is clear from NAR that *being accepted by God for all eternity* and *being ultimately saved* are synonyms. But what if there are no verses that *explicitly* say being accepted by God and being saved are synonyms? We will discover later that *being saved* and *being acceptable to God* are completely different things. Consequently, this point should not be accepted by anyone, universalist or not.

Finally, *it is also not true to say that the universalist today must believe that no one will experience God's punishment.* Christians are no more exempt from divine judgment and the experience of God's remedial chastisement in the afterlife than they are in this life. *God judges and chastises forgiven Christians today.* There is no reason to believe that He will refrain from doing that in the afterlife. If He did choose to *chastise previously forgiven people* in the afterlife, it would not suddenly be contrary to His nature.[2]

Christians are no different in the matters of divine judgment and remedial chastisement than those of other religions. As we will discuss in more detail later, even the apostle Paul expected to be judged for everything he had done during his earthly life when he finally stands before God's Judgment Seat. He believed he

---

[1] 1Cor. 3:15 may be the one exception to this basic principle. It should be observed that the salvation that this verse speaks about takes place after death and, apparently, after someone has been assigned to hell *for a time.* After God's remedial purposes have been accomplished and after the time that it took for those purposes to be fulfilled, he is saved from any further experience of that situation.

[2] 2Sam. 12:1-23. David was forgiven but also chastised by God in several ways afterward.

would experience this judgment[1] even though he had believed in Jesus' death on the cross as a payment for his sins.[2] We have been taught that these two ideas are irreconcilable. But both are clearly held by the apostle Paul.[3]

These are some of the reasons that a person might question NAR's labels. While he might consider himself to have universalist's leanings now, his view of what *Biblical universalism* is may not come close to the one described in NAR. This is the reason that labeling people is so inadequate. The label may only partially fit the person. Guilt by association needs to stop. It is too often the case that many of the most condemning Christians are those who talk the most about grace. I wonder if they really understand the grace that they proclaim.

Is there a Biblical universalism? It seems that there is when one ponders at least some of the available evidence for that perspective. For example, consider a few random verses that lead us in that direction.

> All the people in this world *belong to God.*[4] God *loves* the *whole world* (and not just some supposedly chosen out from the rest of the world to be saved).
> One stands accepted before God *by how he lives* not by what or in whom he has believed.[5]
> All people on earth have been *commanded to praise and worship God.*[6]
> All the people of the earth *pray to the one true God.*[7]
> God's house is a house of prayer *for all nations.*[8]

---

1 Acts 24:14-16, 24-25.
2 1Cor. 15:3-5.
3 Cf., 1Cor. 15:3-5 with Acts 24:14-16, 24-25. For a fuller discussion see my two books, *Acceptable to God without being Saved* and *Freedom through the Cross.*
4 Ps. 24:1.
5 Ps. 24:3-6.
6 Ps. 66:1-4; 67:1-7; Ps. 68:32; 86:9; 96:1-13; 150:6.
7 Ps. 65:2.
8 Isa. 56:6-7; Mk. 11:17. No indication the other nations needed to be proselytes to use it.

All the people of the earth *trust in the one true God.*[1]
All living people on earth will one day *serve the one true God.*[2]
All the living and all the dead will one day *worship the one true God together.*[3]

More could be said, but this has been said in order to show that a rejection of universalism is not as easy as NAR has made it out to be. With a proper understanding of the terms involved[4] and of the real message of the Bible,[5] universalism actually fits with God's original plan for man upon planet earth[6] better than the exclusivism that NAR tries to set forth and defend.

We are certain that God loves the whole world,[7] and that Christ died for the whole world,[8] and that by Christ's death God was reconciled with the whole world.[9] As a result, we are led to ask, "Why would we expect God to be separated from a part of it, large or small, forever?" It seems to be that we ought to expect a universal reunion one day if God has already been reconciled to everyone in the world through the death of His Son.[10]

## Pluralism: An Acceptable Path Shared by Many

According to NAR, belief in Jesus is the only way to get to heaven. Consequently, the suggestion that many different religions could teach a way to be acceptable to God without requiring faith in Jesus would be seen as an anathema by NAR. But if NAR's

---

[1] Ps. 65:5, 8.
[2] Ps. 102:22.
[3] Phil. 2:9-11; Rev. 5:13.
[4] E.g., salvation, save, eternal life, , redemption, justification, justify, and forgiveness.
[5] See my book, *The Prodigal Paradigm*, the Bible's real storyline.
[6] Gen. 1:26, 28; Ps. 8:4-6; Deut. 6:4-9; 10:12-14; Ps. 119:1-3, 7.
[7] John 3:16.
[8] John 1:29; 6:33, 51.
[9] 2Cor. 5:18-20.
[10] 1John 2:2; 4:10. Christ's propitiation was made for the whole world.

understanding of pluralism is tweaked slightly, it will be evident that there is some support for it in the Bible.

Who will ultimately reach heaven? According to NAR, the pluralists give a slightly different answer from the one given by the universalist. It says,

> "Pluralism restricts salvation to *religious people*, regardless of what that religion is. This belief maintains that *all religions are equally valid*, picturing the variety of world religions as *different paths up the same mountain that lead ultimately to the same God*... Unlike universalism, pluralism doesn't require us to allow murderers and drug dealers into heaven, as pluralists still restrict the population of heaven to *religious people*."[1] (emphases mine)

Assuming that NAR's understanding of the pluralists' position is correct, it appears to me both from a reading of my Bible as well as from practical experience that this perspective on life and religion is backwards. I would say that *no religious system*, including Christianity, takes a person *to* God; they all, to some extent, take a person *away from* Him. *Only God's revelation leads a person to God*. Consequently, only God leads a person to God.

Man, for various reasons, consistently confuses the issues involved, complicating the matter, pushing people away from the God who is revealing Himself to all men. The so-called *saved* within Christianity do this[2] as much as the so-called *unsaved* in other religions do it.[3] This is the reason that an infallible, inerrant guide, the Bible, is so important. Without it everyone, including all the Christians and all of the Jews, would be doing whatever is right in his own eyes.

But let's affirm, on the authority of the Bible, that all men,

---

[1] NAR, pp. 44-45.
[2] Cf., Mk. 10:13-16; Matt. 23:15; Gal. 2:11-17.
[3] Cf., Acts 13:6-10; 17:30-34; and (by application at least) Rom. 1:21-25.

around the world, which necessarily encompasses all religions, have some knowledge about the God who created and sustains all things.[1] Let's further affirm, on the authority of the Bible, that all men, including their religious systems, have some revelation of God's will for their lives.[2] Finally, let's affirm that God has given several different means by which forgiveness may be obtained by men around the world. By offering the proper sacrifice in faith, by repenting from one's sins, by being baptized as a first step of repenting of one's sins, by confessing them to God, and by returning to God in love are all ways of obtaining forgiveness according to the Scriptures.[3]

The conclusion that seems apparent is that since all men have some knowledge of God and His will, all men (and their religious systems) have *the potential of leading others to God* as they understand Him from His revelation of Himself. Not every man nor every religious system has been given the same amount of revelation by God. It ought to be expected that God would hold a person accountable for the revelation that has been given to him, and not for the revelation that he has not been given.[4]

But none of this, even in the slightest degree, should be equated with salvation or being saved (or with justification and being justified). Being forgiven and being saved (or being justified) are two different things altogether even though we have been taught the great *assumption* that they are so closely intertwined and involved with one another that they can't be separated from one another. But in the Bible forgiveness is never

---

[1] Rom. 1:18-20.

[2] Ps. 50:6; 97:6-7; John 1:9; Rom. 1:19-20.

[3] See my book *The Grand Spiritual Assumption* for a more in-depth discussion and a more complete list of the ways that God has ordained forgiveness to be obtained. There are at least ten different ways to obtain it, but belief in Jesus is not one of them.

[4] Cf., John 15:22-25.

attached to either salvation or to justification in the way that traditional, orthodox Christianity attaches them.

Remember that NAR is setting before its readers traditional, orthodox, Christian teaching. The same mainline teaching, most likely, that you have been taught. It is the same teaching that I was taught as well. If soteriology had not been so badly formulated, we would not be having trouble seeing the good as well as the bad in the other religions of the world. There are elements of universalism that are good. There are elements of pluralism that are good. But neither offer, nor even broach the subject of, Biblical salvation. That is simply a different discussion.

> *What if* there is such a thing as *God's universal will for all men*?[1]
> *What if* this divine will has been revealed to all men as the standard of behavior that God requires from them to be acceptable to Him?
> *What if* this divine will concerns works even if it also concerns faith?
> *What if* God has ensured man's ability to perform this will as an unconditional benefit of the cross of His Son?
> What if God's divine will is not about getting to heaven when one dies
> And finally, *what if* God's divine will does not require belief in Jesus Christ in order to get to heaven?

Isn't it possible that all men have the potential of using God's revelation to them to help others know Him and live pleasingly before Him?[2] Isn't that the purpose for God giving the revelation in the first place?[3] In this case wouldn't pluralism make better sense and reflect better on the character of God than the exclusivism that NAR is espousing? I think so.

---

[1] See my recent book, *A Shrinking World Requires a Better Christianity.*
[2] Ibid.
[3] Cf., e.g., Ps. 119:9, 11, 105; Ps. 50:6; Ps. 97:6; 2Tim. 3:16-17; John 17:17; etc.

## Inclusivism: A Communion Made Available for All

NAR does not approve of those who attempt to include others who have not trusted in Jesus in the group that God has accepted. Generally speaking, NAR has described inclusivism this way:

> "Inclusivism holds that the sacrificial death of Christ on the cross is *the only means by which* people can be *saved*. However, inclusivism also says that a person can be *saved by Christ without ever personally believing in Christ*. In other words, the death of Christ was sufficient to save a group of people larger than those who have heard and believed in Jesus Christ."[1] (emphases mine)

The key point for our purposes is the idea that *a person can be saved by Christ without ever personally believing in Christ*. As long as NAR understands salvation as getting to heaven after one dies, it will never see the importance of the point that the inclusivist makes here.

*What if* salvation is a deliverance or rescue from personal sins?[2]

*What if* salvation is a deliverance or rescue from the present evil age that we have to live within?[3]

*What if* salvation is a deliverance or rescue of believers in Christ from the coming Tribulation?[4]

*What if* salvation is a deliverance or rescue of people physically at a future time so that they can enter the Kingdom that Jesus has returned to earth to establish?[5]

*What if* salvation turns out never to be a deliverance or rescue from hell to heaven?

NAR, using Acts 16:30-31, *assumes* that salvation, which according to its teachings is a once-for-all deliverance or rescue from hell to heaven, can only be obtained through believing in

---

[1] NAR, p. 45.
[2] Matt. 1:21.
[3] Acts 2:40; Gal. 1:4.
[4] 1Thess. 4:13—5:11, esp. 5:9-10.
[5] John 12:47; Matt. 24:13-14.

Jesus. I had continued to believe this understanding of Acts 16:31 until very recently. But the more my understanding grows, the more I comprehend that such an interpretation can't be what the original author had in mind when he wrote Paul's reply in answer to the Philippian jailer's question.

Why can't the term *saved* in Acts 16:30-31 refer to a deliverance from hell to heaven? Well, for one thing, it *never* means that! For another, the immediate context doesn't give us any indication that such an interpretation is valid or that such an idea was ever on Luke's or Paul's mind. Also, the message of the Bible is not about sharing the right message about a path to heaven. It is about walking with the God of heaven while accomplishing His will upon earth in this life.

NAR has *assumed* that salvation is about going to heaven when a person dies. Then it also *assumes* that *this salvation* can *only* be obtained by faith in Jesus. With these two *assumptions* as its foundation, it concludes that no one gets to heaven without believing in Jesus.

That would make sense *if* salvation were about obtaining heaven and *if* the salvation referenced here *can only be obtained* through faith in Jesus. But neither *assumption* is true. Salvation never refers to going to heaven or obtaining a heavenly destiny. And the salvation that is described here, apparently, can be obtained without faith in Jesus.[1]

A central and basic premise of the inclusivist is given by Sanders,[2] who is an inclusivist himself. It is amazing how many people

---

[1] John 12:47. How could all the world have been saved at Jesus' first advent if most of the world had never heard of Him? Obviously, the salvation referred to here could not be based upon having faith in Jesus; it must be based upon being acceptable to God apart from ever having faith in Jesus.

[2] NAR is quoting from John Piper's book, *Jesus The Only Way to God*, p. 27 which uses Sanders as a representative and proponent of inclusivism.

miss his simple but profound observation. He says,

> "It is **not certain** ... that one must hear of Christ in this life to obtain **salvation.** [New Testament passages used by Sanders but not quoted in NAR] simply say there is no other way one can **get to heaven** except through the work of Christ; **they do not say one has to know about that work in order to benefit from the work.**"[1] (emphasis and bracket mine)

Sanders' first statement is 100% true if salvation is understood Biblically.[2] One does not need to know about Jesus in order to experience some of the salvations listed on page twenty-three earlier. But if Christian orthodoxy is the plumb line for determining what is true, Sanders' first statement would be 100% false because salvation would then necessarily refer to a deliverance from hell to heaven.

His second statement is 100% false since the work of Christ on the cross was not for the purpose of getting anyone to heaven. His assumption would then be identical to NAR's assumption. In that case, both would be unfounded.

His third statement is 100% true since forgiveness, for example, is based upon the accomplishments of a cross about which a person may have no information even though he trusts in God to forgive him. This is the portrayal of all of the offers of forgiveness in the OT. Forgiveness was granted, but there is no evidence that it was granted because of a person's faith in Jesus (or in a coming Messiah). There are other benefits of the cross as well that all men enjoy even though they might not have ever heard of the cross or had been taught about its significance.[3]

---

[1] Ibid, p. 47.

[2] See Acts 16:30-31. Notice that everyone has to *assume* that the salvation in these verses are a reference to going to heaven and that they are the *universal standard* for any and every salvation.

[3] See my book, *Freedom through the Cross* for a discussion of these benefits.

Inclusivism has made a significant point: *one doesn't need to know about or believe in the cross to benefit from it.* If one doesn't have to believe in Jesus to be saved (in the Biblical sense of salvation rather than in the theological sense foisted upon the term), then NAR's defense of the need to believe in Jesus to be saved (in the theological sense rather than the Biblical sense) is a futile one.

Before we side with either NAR or Sanders, the proponent of inclusivism, it is important to remember that neither Sanders nor NAR has proven that salvation is about going to heaven or about a guarantee of a heavenly destiny. The identity of salvation is the critical point in this discussion. At this point both are mistaken about that meaning. As a result, all of the debate between them is futile and meaningless. Neither can win this debate.

But Sanders' point about the benefits of the cross reaching those who have never heard of Jesus or believed in Him is a great contribution. Consequently, there is something to like from inclusivism just like there is from universalism and pluralism. Unfortunately for NAR, the benefits from these other three viewpoints tend to reveal the errors of exclusivism. The case that NAR attempts to make has trusted more in dogmatism than expositional proof up to this point. Assumptions and conjectures don't turn into facts by a rational defense of them

.

## Exclusivism: All of the Blessings for the Privileged Few

The fourth and final worldview attempting to identify the people who will populate heaven is designated by NAR as exclusivism. When NAR expounds this view, it makes it clear that only Christianity is exclusive because only Christianity has a Savior that is able to deliver a person from the prospect of hell. It says,

"Exclusivism is the view that *salvation* is *limited to those who exercise personal faith in Jesus Christ as their Savior*. Unlike universalists, exclusivists believe *many – actually most – people will be condemned to an eternity in hell*. Unlike pluralists, exclusivists believe that hell will be populated by *sincere followers of other religions*."[1] (emphases mine)

These are the cold, icy convictions that will eventually sink the titanic of Christian soteriology represented in NAR. In our shrinking world we need a much better message than this one because the *objective investigator* will not find this view in the Bible accurately describing most of the rest of the world. Christians are beginning to question the orthodox use of grace because the world around them doesn't make sense if the traditional view represented in NAR is true.

More and more people want to see the message *explicitly* spelled out for them from the Scriptures. The window for accepting *assumptions* and *conjectures* such as NAR presents is fast closing as many religious surveys affirm. The only way to construct the message that NAR tries to defend from the Scriptures is to *cut and paste* passages together that say things close to what is needed. But no passage actually teaches it all or even the heart of the so-called *gospel of grace* message.

Because our world is shrinking today, most of us know enough people from several different cultures and religions that seem to fit the demands of the Scriptures for those rightly related to God. The pontifications of Christian pundits, of course, say this can't be true. What a person may think is true, might be, in fact, the furthest thing from the truth. Appearances can deceive. All that, of course, is true.

But most readers of this book know people from other

[1] Ibid, p. 47.

religious faiths or backgrounds who are better adherents to the principles of Christianity than many of the Christians that they know. Some of these people you've known your whole life, and would have less hesitation to vouch for their relation to God, even though they don't believe exactly like you do, than for some confirmed Christians in the Christian community.

What NAR teaches is disturbing on two fronts. First, some of the key beliefs it sets forth can't be proven from the Scriptures to the objective mind. That is the reason that NAR has to make so many *assumptions* along the way. What it needs said is simply not present in the proof texts that it uses.

Second, some of NAR's proposals portray God in a very, very bad light. *Christianity's god doesn't seem to be any better than the radical Muslim's god except that the Christian's God chooses to carry out all of His destruction after death rather than during this life.* That is not a very admirable thing to say about a God who is supposed to be perfect in every way, a God who loves the entire world and not just some special individuals picked out from the rest of the world.

*The one true God is supposed to be a God who is just like Jesus.* When questioned concerning the greatest of all commandments, He taught that all of God's requirements "hang on" (i.e., can be summed up in) two commands: *love God and love your neighbor as yourself.*[1] Since that is true, how much revelation does God need to give to those outside the Judeo-Christian faith stream for them to live acceptable lives before Him? The obvious answer is "not much!"

The Scriptures that NAR offers to support what it believes are the classic passages that most Christians have learned or heard

---

[1] Matt. 22:34-40.

preached since early childhood. Because of space, I won't quote them here, but you must look them up to see if they prove what NAR proposes to be true. Those verses are John 3:16; John 11:25-26; Acts 16:31 and Rom. 10:9. Do these passages support any of the following principles:

> That *salvation* is *limited* to those who exercise *personal faith in Jesus* Christ as their Savior;[1]
> That *most people* will be *condemned* to hell for as long as they have an existence;
> That hell will be populated by *sincere followers of other religions*;[2]
> That individuals in every culture must personally trust in Jesus Christ as their Savior from hell in order *to be in a right relationship* with God;[3]
> That *eternal salvation* is connected to *personal belief*.[4]

Closeness doesn't count in Biblical exegesis. The Bible either *explicitly* delineates a concept, or it doesn't. Not only is NAR's theology about salvation based upon extremely poor exegesis, its basic premise, that there is a path given in the Scriptures that leads a person to heaven, must be read into the Bible before it can be found there. Since we will deal with each of these verses in the following discussions, it will be helpful for the reader to make a list of what these verses actually say and of what is *assumed* to be true in these verses.

> For example, does John 3:16 even broach the subject of heaven, or of forgiveness, or of hell?

---

[1] Remember that *salvation* refers to going to heaven and *Savior* refers to a deliverer from hell. If the author of NAR had not made salvation a heaven-hell issue but had allowed salvation to relate to this life and the future kingdom of Messiah in this life, we would have been more receptive to this point, generally speaking.

[2] Are these last two principles even addressed in the passages NAR offered in support of orthodox Christianity (John 3:16; 11:25-26; Acts 16:31; Rom. 10:9)?

[3] Remember that being in *a right relationship with God* and *being saved* are two different things altogether, Biblically speaking. This will be confirmed in a later chapter.

[4] All of these principles come from pp. 47-48 just before the supporting verses are given.

What does *perish* mean in the immediate context of John 3:16?

What does the apostle John mean when he uses the phrase *eternal life*?

After answering those questions, don't be surprised if you discover that John 3:16 doesn't say anything remotely similar to what you've heard all of your life. *Many Christian writers present their theology in their exposition rather than the mind of the author of Scripture.*

Before moving on to the messages that Jesus, Peter, and Paul actually preached, we need . . .

to take a brief look at the importance that Christianity places upon believing in Jesus as the only path that leads to heaven,

to clarify the distinctions between justification and salvation,

to demonstrate how an impressive, rational defense of Christian exclusivism may be worthless, and

to outline the basic meanings of the central terms used in the debate before us.

So let us begin.

# Chapter 2

# The Importance of the Belief
# That Jesus is the Only Way to Heaven

Although there is much to be considered in all three of the other world views, NAR believes that only one view fits Christianity as the Reformers handed it down to us. Just how important is the doctrine of believing in Jesus as the only means of getting to heaven? For NAR it is all-important. *Supposedly* it is the foundation for everything that makes Christianity distinctive.

The *gospel of grace* makes Christianity different from all the other religions of the world. That gospel, according to NAR, is simply the belief that faith alone in Christ alone is the way into heaven. Without this belief in an exclusive grace, Christianity becomes invisible, camouflaged among the rest of the religions of the world and indistinguishable from them. Consequently, NAR summarizes the perceived apostasy within the Christian churches with this analysis:

> "Christians are waffling, wavering, and in the process of ceding *the bedrock belief of historic Christianity*: Salvation is only available through faith in Jesus Christ."[1] (emphasis mine)

The reader must be careful to stay focused upon the *exact statements* used by NAR because its arguments are only as good as its statements are factual. NAR's arguments are built upon the premise that, generally speaking, the major salvific terms used in the Bible refer to the same thing. How does that help NAR's defense

---

[1] NAR, p. 22.

of the doctrine that faith in Jesus is the only path by which a person can obtain heaven? If justification and salvation refer to the same thing, generally speaking, then there is no harm in applying what the Scriptures say about justification to the topic of salvation, and vice versa. Consequently, *to be saved is to be justified, and to be justified is to be saved.* You can't have one without the other. If salvation involves the matter of a deliverance from hell and a gift of an eternal destiny in heaven, then justification in some way or other must involve or secure those things too. And, more importantly, if salvation is apart from any work on man's part, as NAR *assumes* is true, then justification must fit within the same parameters. For example, works simply can't be involved with either. In short, by equating all of these terms, NAR has more material to work with as it attempts to defend the exclusivity of Christianity.

## Interchangeable Words and Descriptions

NAR says, "Salvation is *only* available through faith in Jesus Christ." All Christians trained in the accepted orthodoxy of their faith agree on this point.[1] And *faith in Jesus Christ* also obtains eternal life, right?[2] That must mean that salvation, faith in Jesus Christ, and eternal life are vitally connected. Consequently, one of the *assumptions* that is formulated is that salvation is the obtainment of eternal life.

But is this assumption legitimate? Haven't we subtly reversed the point of the terms? Doesn't salvation refer to a deliverance or a rescue from someone or something? But the way in which we

---

[1] Acts 16:31. But it is time to ask the question, "Does the context support the *assumptions* that typically undergird the popular understanding of this verse?"

[2] John 3:16; 6:47; etc.

are using salvation in the assumption above is that salvation is not a deliverance or rescue *from* something, but a gift *to* someone. This is subtle to be sure, but that is the reason this assumption has been accepted for so long. The truth of the matter is that salvation and the initial reception of the gift of (or access to) eternal life are two very different things. This distinction will be demonstrated as we move along.

Furthermore, most are unaware that in the commonly accepted approach, eternal life has been redefined just as salvation has, departing from its Biblical meaning. NAR teaches that eternal life refers to a life and residence with God in heaven forever.[1] This might have some legitimacy if the meaning of eternal life had anything to do with a promise of heaven. But it doesn't. In fact, neither salvation nor eternal life has any Biblical reference to heaven or to a heavenly destiny. These facts ought to suggest to the reader that a complete rethinking of our soteriology is needed.

NAR never defines eternal life for its readers anywhere in the book.[2] It also *assumes* that salvation is somehow connected with going to heaven when a person dies. The more undefined or mis-defined the terms are, the more they can mean whatever the interpreter needs them to mean.

NAR makes sure that its readers know that eternal life comes from believing in Jesus. But it lets its readers *assume* that salvation is about obtaining heaven as a free gift and that eternal life is also about going to heaven when a person dies. With these two

---

[1] NAR, pp. 25-26.

[2] The reader should write down on a sheet of paper the terms eternal life, salvation, justification, the kingdom of heaven, and the gospel. Under each term he should write down his understanding of that term in as brief a statement as possible. Then under each of his definitions, he should write out a verse(s) that explicitly gives his understanding of the term. Do they match? Or have you found that you need to tweak the verse in order to make it say what needs to be said to support your definition of the term?

*assumptions,* the classic view of Christianity, that NAR sets forth, makes both salvation and eternal life say more than the Bible intends them to say. By loading these terms with meanings that they cannot bear, NAR makes its readers believe that they get more out of their faith in Jesus than they actually do. Neither salvation nor eternal life has anything to do with the obtainment of heaven as a free gift from God. That may be part of Christianity's *gospel of grace,* but it isn't part of the message of the Bible.

> *What if* Christianity's supposition about the need of the world is wrong? It *assumes* that the great need is to miss hell and make one's way to heaven instead.
>
> *What if* Christianity doesn't offer a solution to this supposed need as it *assumes* that it does? Isn't it plain that the result of Christianity's message could require assurances to be given by Christian preachers and teachers that they really have no authority to give?

Add to these two points one further one: *what if* a great deal of the problem is the confusion propagated by the various surveys on Christianity? These surveys are supposed to test the orthodoxy of the Christianity that is current in the locale in which the survey is taken.

> *What if* the *orthodoxy* of the surveys is actually unscriptural?
>
> *What if* the terms used in the surveys were incorrectly defined?
>
> *What if* eternal life has nothing to do with going to heaven when a person dies?
>
> *What if* the survey had asked, "Can many religions teach a person how to be *acceptable to God* and *prepare him for his final judgment in heaven?*" Would the answers given by those surveyed be truthful then?

Of course, what is *assumed* to be orthodox Christian theology would answer that question with a fervent "No!" But does the Bible support that orthodoxy? If it isn't supported, what should it be called then? Heterodoxy? Or just plain heresy?

Being acceptable to God and being prepared now for your final judgment describe an entirely different matter than being saved or receiving eternal life (or being justified). Christianity has traditionally *assumed* that there is no difference between those issues. The surveys have *assumed* that there is no difference between those ideas. If we let someone interchange terms that are not synonyms of one another, we will be led to draw the wrong conclusions. We need to pay attention to what exactly is being said. To assume that salvation, eternal life (according to the orthodox Christian perspective), and being acceptable to God are the same thing is to miss the teaching of the Bible completely. And we have done exactly that!

## Is Heaven only for Christians?

When NAR asks, "Is *heaven* reserved *exclusively for Christians*, or are there *multiple paths to God*?" it is relying upon several *assumptions* being true.

> It is *assuming* that the Bible focuses upon going to heaven and that it explains how a person can get there.
> It is *assuming* that a path to God is the same as a path to heaven in the Bible.
> It is *assuming* that going to heaven must have something to do with believing in Jesus.
> It is *assuming* that the teachings of the various religions focus upon explaining how to get to heaven.
> It is *assuming* that salvation is about going to heaven.
> It is *assuming* that being acceptable to God is the same thing as being saved.
> It is also *assuming* that being right or righteous before God is impossible apart from faith in Jesus Christ.

Can you prove that all of these assumptions are true from *explicit*

Biblical passages? You should attempt to do this. What was the result? Will it make a difference in your life and in how you view others, especially those of other faiths?

When NAR asks, "Is heaven reserved exclusively for Christians," all Christians ought to be shocked. When we aren't, what it says about us is not flattering. And when NAR answers its own question with a resounding, "Yes!" they ought to be even more dismayed. The verses that traditional Christian apologetics uses to prove that Jesus limited heaven to those who believe in Him, will be shown to prove otherwise. Jesus never gave any means, roads or otherwise, of obtaining a heavenly destiny. *As a result, it will prove futile for anyone to look for a path that was never provided to a destination that was never offered.* Not explicitly at least.

As NAR represents mainline Christian thinking, it offers two proofs for its warning that to reject Jesus as *the only way* to heaven is to have *no way* to heaven for yourself. For what has become the accepted soteriology of the Christian faith, this is an either-or situation. Either a person believes in Jesus to get to heaven, or he is not able to ever get there.

NAR first illustrates the rationale for the exclusivism that it defends, then it gives a couple of verses to support it Biblically. Let's look at the illustration now to see if it properly sets forth the exclusivity of the gospel of Christ. The two verses that NAR uses to support its argument will be used again and again throughout the book so we will have other occasions to analyze those verses.

### An illustration of Christian Exclusiveness

If a person is trying to get to Houston, Texas from Dallas, Texas but takes Interstate 75 north by mistake, he will never get to Houston regardless of how long he stays on that road. Even though he may recognize that he is on the wrong road, unless he gets on the right road, he will never arrive in Houston.

The conclusion that NAR reaches in its analogy is obviously correct. But is its analogy a good one? Does it fit the Biblical information that we have been given?

For the analogy to work with what we know the Bible actually says, we would have to change the desired destination from Houston, Texas to Cuba. Finding *a paved road* that leads to Cuba (or any island will work: the Azores Islands, Greenland, etc.) fits the Biblical material better than getting to Houston, Texas from Dallas, Texas.

The point is simply that *there is no paved road that can carry you to Cuba*. Such a road does not exist. Obviously, no one can travel a road that doesn't exist.

NAR's analogy reflects the theology of Christianity perfectly, but it does not fit the Biblical message because that message never connects salvation with either heaven or hell. God has not promised a heavenly destination nor given *a road* to get there. Consequently, it will be impossible to find such a road in the Scriptures, regardless of how long you look for it.

# Chapter 3

# Are We Talking about Justification or Salvation?

Good, clear, and accurate communication in marriage is about the most difficult assignment a couple has to fulfill with each other in order to have a happy and fulfilling married life. After fifty years of marriage to the same wonderful lady, my wife and I are still working on this obstacle called communication. Maybe you can relate a bit to a not-so-uncommon exchange between us (but I'll use the third person to protect the innocent).

One day a husband asks his wife if she knows Mr. Albertson. That is a fairly simple, direct question, he mistakenly thinks to himself. She responds to the question this way:

> "No. But I know his wife and their four children. She is a lovely person. She is kind, thoughtful, and very patient. She is also extremely smart and very wise. Their kids are well-liked, well-mannered, and doing well in school."

Although I've shortened the wife's response for the sake of space, you get the idea I'm sure (at least I'm sure that all the husbands get the point). Most husbands would respond to this wife's remarks by rhetorically asking, "What?" At that point the wife adds more of the same kind of very informative facts as she had before but now with illustrations from conversations that she has had with other families who are mutual friends with you and the person about whom you're seeking information. All the facts that she had previous delineated are confirmed.

Bewildered, the husband walks away disappointed. Can you guess the reason for his bewilderment and disappointment? What has the wife assumed here? She has assumed that the husband and wife, because of their close relationship (after all, they are living in the same house and raising the same children!), must possess the same virtues. But the husband sees this as little more than assumption based upon indirect evidence. The husband walks away from the conversation, thinking that he has no more sound, verifiable, indisputable information than he had before his conversation began.

What does the Bible mean when it refers to a person as *being right before God*? What do most interpreters *assume* to be true about justification? The importance of *being right before God* really centers on both the *means* for being justified and the *result* of being *justified*. NAR concludes,

> "The issue of the exclusivity of the gospel … is key to answering life's most important question: 'How can a man be *in the right* before God?' (Job 9:2)"

Why is it surprising that NAR chooses Job's comment to speak to the problem of the exclusivity of the gospel? Did Job know anything about NAR's gospel? The book of Job is believed by many scholars to be the earliest book of the Bible, probably written even before the time of Abraham. There is no evidence in the Scriptures that Job knew anything about a coming Messiah. God's revelations that His Messiah would die for the sins of the world, that He would be sinless, born of a virgin, born in Bethlehem, and that He would be the king of the whole world were not given for another twelve to fifteen hundred years after Job's time. The prophets that reveal these truths didn't live until the eighth century B.C. at the earliest.

What would "being in the right before God" have meant to Job? Does Job answer his own question? If he does, is Job's answer the same one that NAR is trying to defend? Or is NAR's theological grid completely unknown to Job whose only concern is *his experiential relationship with God*? In the book of Job we have to conclude that neither Job nor God had any concern for the gospel of grace that NAR defends.

God declares Job's own guiltlessness[1] even though God has, at times, stricken both the guiltless as well as the wicked in this earthly life. Consequently, Job's trial has come upon him at a time when God Himself had previously declared him to be *a blameless individual who fears God and turns away from evil.*[2] How can NAR use Job to represent a person who is in need of Jesus? The *right standing* that Job is talking about is the divine approval of his *walk* with God, not some once-for-all, forensic acquittal by God of a man who was heretofore irretrievable in his own sinfulness.

Is it not possible that God made different ways for different people to be "in the right" (Biblically speaking) before Him? Rom. 2:13 gives one way to be in the right before God. Rom. 1:19-20 gives another way to be in the right before God. Rom. 3:28 gives still another way to be right before God. If God had only one way to be "in the right" before Him, and if He didn't make that way available to all men, then *God* says of Himself that He would be an unjust Judge, showing favoritism.[3]

In case you didn't follow that, let me restate it for you this way: if NAR is correct in holding the conviction that belief in Jesus is the only way to heaven, then God shows partiality in His judgment over all mankind. If NAR is correct, then God is not a just judge over the whole world. He would not be *the God of all*

---

[1] Job 9:21-22. This point is contrary to NAR's assumption that all men are guilty before God unless they believe the gospel of grace centering upon Jesus' person and work.
[2] Job. 1:8.
[3] Rom. 2:11-13; 3:29-30; 9:30-33.

*men* (as Paul declared that He is). This divinely revealed truth is almost always missed or conveniently ignored. God would only be *the God of some*.[1] We would do well to meditate upon the fact that it is the apostle Paul, writing under the inspiration of the Holy Spirit who says that *God is the God of all,* having the same requirement for all in order to protect His impartiality as a just Judge. God only judges people on the information that they have, not on the information that others have but they don't have. To most of us that makes perfect sense.

NAR is at a loss to explain the reason that so many are no longer believing the doctrine of the exclusivity of the gospel of Jesus Christ as they once did. The traditional Christian position presented by NAR remains convinced, however, that ...

> "Jesus and the New Testament writers ... consistently taught that faith in Christ is the only means by which anyone can be *saved*."[2]

At one time in the past I would have been in full agreement with that statement. But when you study every use of the terms *save* and *salvation* (and justify and justification) and when you determine to what those terms basically refer, you are forced to change your opinion. There are salvations described in the Bible that don't involve belief in Jesus. When these salvations are simply and clearly set before us, they challenge our thinking and lead us to broaden our perspective on the relationship that people around the world might have with the one true God.

Remember that I pointed out earlier how easily passages on justification and passages on salvation can be wrongly used to support each other? NAR is using that assumption that there is little difference between justification and salvation again here.

---

[1] Rom. 3:29-30.
[2] NAR, p. 26.

NAR begins by using Job to ask, "How can a man be *in the right before God*?" but then it continues its argument speaking about *salvation*. It is *assuming* that justification, being in the right before God, is the same thing as salvation, being delivered from something, namely, hell. NAR *assumes* that these two terms or concepts are intertwined in meaning. A careful study of the Bible will reveal that they are not intertwined or even connected in the way that NAR claims them to be.

I don't know the reason that others are relinquishing the doctrine that teaches that Jesus is the only way to heaven. But I know the reason that I have relinquished that doctrine. And that reason is so extremely simple. As I independently studied for the last fourteen years these terms and the issues related to them, I found that *the Bible does not teach that salvation is about going to heaven!* Become a Christian if you will, but you won't be any closer to heaven than you were before you became one. I hope that you discover a better reason for trusting in Jesus than *supposing* that He will get you to heaven when you die. He won't get you to heaven, nor will He keep you from your own personal judgment.

As NAR offers its suggestions for the reason that so many are giving up the doctrine of Christ being the exclusive way to heaven, it *assumes* that the various salvific terms are basic synonyms. For example, God's plan of *redemption*, God's prescribed way of *forgiveness*, the need for *reconciliation*,[1] *eternal salvation*,[2] and *the road that leads to heaven*[3] are all synonyms and, therefore, can be used interchangeably. Since NAR never offers proof that they are synonyms or that they refer to a person's eternal, heavenly destiny, it begs the question to *assume* that they can all be

---

[1] NAR, p. 27. The first three of these terms or phrases are found on this page.
[2] Ibid, p. 32.
[3] Ibid, p. 38.

interchanged without corrupting the message being given.

Not only are salvation and justification not equivalents, neither one gets anyone to heaven after he dies. A driver's license is required to drive a car legally. A pilot's license is required to fly an aircraft. But these are different government approvals altogether. Regardless of the similarities between the two licenses, they are not the same; they are not interchangeable; they are not equivalents.

If you have one, that particular license does not permit you to operate the other vehicle legally. No amount of testimony, regardless of how logical or how rational it may be, can turn a driver's license into a pilot's license or vise versa.

In the same way, justification and salvation are wonderful things. But they are not interchangeable; they are not equivalents. The Bible is clear that one can be saved (in the Biblical sense of that term) without being justified (in NAR's theological sense), and that he can be justified (in the Biblical sense of that term) without being saved (in NAR's understanding of that term). Just because a person has experienced one, there is no Biblical reason to believe he must have also experienced the other. The Bible doesn't support these theological constructions.

To keep to our analogy of two licenses, justification and salvation are *assumed* to be like the pilot's license in NAR's theology. They both get you into the air (or get you to heaven). But with that *assumption* as to their function and intent, one quickly learns that neither works very well on earth; neither has much to do with moving a person through life. NAR admits this fact in various ways throughout its discussions.

The message that is typically given by pastors, teachers, and evangelists today focuses upon the eternal destiny of the person being witnessed to. But the message of the Bible actually places the focus upon something else entirely.

The typical message we hear today gives its hearers an assurance of going to heaven and avoiding all consequences of a life that might have been less than God desired from them. But the message of the Bible is not focused upon the afterlife as much as we have been made to think. Once we become emotionally detached from that message about the afterlife, a message, by the way, that produces much guilt and uncertainty for a great many Christians, we are ready to learn about what was actually on God's mind when He first gave His revelation to the penmen of the NT. That message will meet every need we have completely, abundantly, and gloriously.

# Chapter 4

# Without Exclusivism Christianity Collapses?

NAR gives six essential doctrines of Christianity that, in its opinion, logically collapse if the exclusivity of *belief in Jesus Christ as the only way to heaven* is proven false. Those doctrines are as follows:

1. Absolute truth no longer exists.
2. The Bible is no longer an authoritative, trustworthy guide.
3. Christ can no longer be divine.
4. There is no need for Christ's death on the cross.
5. The doctrine of eternal punishment for rejecters of Christ is lost.
6. The missions enterprise is greatly hampered.

I would like to assure the reader that none of these six doctrines will collapse as NAR fears if the exclusivity of the gospel of Christ is proven to be false. Since men, rather than God, have formulated and promoted the exclusivism that NAR is trying to defend, none of these doctrines is destroyed or impugned in the least by the complete rejection of Christian exclusivism. *NAR's formulation of the gospel of grace is simply not Biblical.* NAR's doctrine of exclusivism is itself based upon an extensively thorough misunderstanding of the message of the Bible (and the terms used to communicate the true message).

I suspect that many will want at least some feedback about specific reasons that these doctrines are not in danger. So, very briefly let me say a few words about them. If Jesus never said what NAR believes that He said, then all of the problems that NAR imagines are only of its own creation. But did Jesus ever really teach the belief that NAR is trying to defend? When the verses are actually examined in the upcoming chapters, it will become obvious that Jesus never taught the exclusivism that NAR is attempting to establish for future generations.

There is a classic movie that probably everyone is familiar with or at least should be because it is such a great movie. It is called *Princess Bride*. Near the end of the movie, the hero comes to rescue his true love from the clutches of the evil prince. He is trying to get to the castle before his love is forced to marry the evil prince. But he arrives just moments after the officiate ends the ceremony and pronounces them husband and wife.

When the hero's bride bemoans the fact that he is too late because the ceremony has already taken place, he asks her if she ever said, "I do"? She said no she didn't. It was obvious that she was too much in shock at the time. Then the hero concludes, *"If you never said it (namely, 'I do,') then you are not married. If you didn't say it (i.e., "I do "), then it (the marriage) didn't happen."*

That is the basic approach that we will take to all six of NAR's fears of a collapsing Christian faith if belief in Jesus as the only way to heave is denied. Just like in *Princess Bride*, if Jesus "never said it (namely, that belief in Him was the only way to heaven), denying that He said it (i.e., that belief in Him is the only way to heaven) doesn't affect Christianity in any way whatever." So let's take a quick look at each of the six essential doctrines of Christianity that NAR fears will be overturned if Christian exclusivism is denied.

## Absolute Truth no longer Exists

NAR believes, as do I, that there are universal principles that apply to all peoples in all ages. There is truth; there is error. And, as one ought to expect, the God of truth explains which is which. When God speaks on a matter, He doesn't stutter! He speaks plainly and definitively. What He says is authoritative and true. But if we misinterpret and, thereby, misunderstand what Jesus said, our poor handling of God's Word not only misrepresents the Bible, but it gives the world a reason to deny the Bible's truthfulness because all errors will eventually be exposed.

The problem with NAR's hypothesis is that it tries to turn an idea that is *not true* into an *absolute, universal truth* for all people. Consequently, NAR says,

> "Faith in Jesus Christ as Savior as the exclusive way of **salvation** is an absolute truth *for all people.*"[1] (emphasis mine)

We must disagree with NAR on several points relative to its declaration. First, salvation never refers to a deliverance from hell accompanied by a guaranteed ticket to heaven. Such an idea is never *explicitly* affirmed anywhere in the Bible. Second, the salvations that Jesus offered have been offered elsewhere in the Bible without requiring belief in Him, even as a coming Messiah, as we will see in a moment.

But if Jesus never said that belief in Him would result in a guaranteed, heavenly destiny, then to expose and dismiss a promise that was never given in the first place would produce no negative effect at all on the truthfulness of the Bible. *If Jesus never said it, then to deny that Jesus ever said it is doing the right thing. This denial actually guards the Bible's integrity. NAR is simply putting into Jesus' mouth a promise that He never gave to anyone.* Indirectly, rejecting a claim that Jesus never made bolsters the existence of absolute truth by denying to an error the status of absolute truth.

---

[1] Ibid, p. 50.

*NAR has assumed that Jesus said something that He never said.* It tries to turn what Jesus said into more than He said. This fact is the foundation for rejecting all six of NAR's propositions. By the end of this book, the reader should be well instructed on the proper understanding of the classic verses that have been taken out of their contexts to support the mistaken belief that faith in Jesus is the only way to heaven.

## The Bible Is no longer Authoritative or Trustworthy

NAR believes that the rejection of Jesus as the only way to heaven destroys the authority and trustworthiness of the Bible. That would be correct *if* the Bible ever made the claim that belief in Jesus was the only way to heaven. But since the Bible never *explicitly* says that faith in Jesus Christ is the only way to heaven, it is impossible to lower or destroy the Bible's authority or trustworthiness by disproving Christianity's claim to have an exclusive way into heaven through faith in Jesus. I am simply making a distinction between what the Bible teaches and what NAR is suggesting. These are not the same thing.

## The Divinity of Jesus Is no longer Possible

According to NAR, the doctrine of the Christ's deity is dependent upon the exclusivity of faith in Jesus as the only path to heaven.[1] NAR reasons that if Jesus declares that He is the only way to heaven, then if that declaration is disproven, He either lied or lacked one of the necessary attribute of deity called omniscience.[2] In either case, Jesus would necessarily be less than divine.

But *what if* the problem is all ours?

---

[1] NAR, p. 52.
[2] Ibid, p. 53.

*What if* Jesus never actually made that claim at all?

*What if* that claim was constructed by well-meaning, but misguided men?

In such a situation, it would be quite clear that a denial of the doctrine that faith in Jesus is the only way into heaven would not impugn His character at all. If Jesus never said it, His divinity cannot be impugned for *not* having said it. Let me illustrate.

Let's say that some people try to convince the rest that Jesus taught the view that the world is flat. Today we know that such a view is erroneous. Denying that view of the world, if Jesus had actually affirmed it, would impugn Jesus' character. But if Jesus never said the world is flat, then to deny that the world is flat would have no negative impact upon Jesus at all.

The classic verses that NAR uses to support its claim that Jesus did, in fact, claim to be the exclusive way to heaven will be carefully analyzed in chapters seven and eight. From NAR's point of view, these verses overturn all three of the other worldviews that offer alternative suggestions as to who will make it to heaven. According to NAR, the universalist won't make it; the pluralist won't make it; the inclusivist won't make it.

But a proper understanding of the verses that NAR uses to support its position yields a far different conclusion than the one NAR has drawn. Understanding these verses in their immediate contexts will yield an entirely different interpretation than the one NAR draws.

I was taught early in my ministry that it is fairly easy to make the Bible *say* almost anything a person would like it to say. But he can't make it *teach* what he would like it to say. When we take verses out of their contexts or give the terms different meanings than the Bible gives them, we can make the Bible *say* things that it really doesn't *teach* when analyzed properly and taken as a whole. My advice to the reader is this: *Don't let the theology that you have learned keep you from the truth of the Scriptures.* I did for almost thirty-five years. Now I have to play catch-up.

## The Atonement Is no longer Necessary

The fourth doctrine that NAR fears will collapse if Jesus is proven not to be the exclusive way to heaven is the need for Christ's death on the cross (which NAR mistakenly refers to it as an atonement). First of all, look up the word atonement and see if it is ever *explicitly* used of Jesus' death on the cross. It isn't. Jesus' death was not an atonement! His death provided forgiveness, a *taking away* or a complete *removal* of sin. That is different from a *covering* for sin. The concepts of atoning and forgiving are not synonyms. It is not helpful, but rather quite confusing, to claim that they are equivalents. If they were the same, verses in the book of Leviticus would be quite redundant.[1]

Christians have been exposed almost entirely to a false message about Jesus getting people to heaven. Consequently, if Jesus isn't the exclusive means of getting someone there, then His death was cruel and meaningless, according to NAR. But . . .

*What if* Jesus' death doesn't get anyone to heaven?

*What if* God the Father's design and intent of His Son's cross was to do other things rather than to secure heavenly destinies for those who believe in Jesus?

*What if* His death provides for the forgiveness of sins so that a person can walk with God the Father? Would the Father still be mean and cruel to send Jesus to the cross?

*What if* His death breaks the bondage that indwelling sin would have had over every person so that each one can walk with God and express faith in Him? Would His death still be useless?

---

[1] Cf., Lev. 4:20ff.

*What if* His death broke the bondage to Satan that would have been created when each person sins his first sin? Would His death still be useless?

*What if* His death forever destroyed the daily death that is the consequence of each man's first sin so that death no longer defines anyone? Because of the work of the cross on behalf of all mankind, freedom and hope define all men (or should). Would His death still be meaningless because it doesn't also get a person to heaven?

Properly understood then, the death of Christ is the basis for all of God's dealings with the entire world. Some of the things it accomplished are unconditional, that is to say, they are applied to all men directly and immediately without requiring any response in return. Some of the things that the cross accomplished are conditional. They will benefit only the person who seeks them in faith. But the cross was necessary for so much more than giving powerful reasons for believing in Jesus. Consequently, the cross of Christ Jesus remains central to life even when the exclusivism of belief in Jesus as the only way to heaven is denied.

## Hell no longer Exists for Unbelievers

The fifth doctrine that NAR is afraid will collapse, if the exclusivism of the gospel of Jesus Christ (i.e., that belief in Jesus is the only way to get to heaven) is denied or proven to be an error, is that there will be no punishment in hell for those who reject Jesus. I am not suggesting that there is no hell; nor am I suggesting that no one will go to hell. Nothing could be further from the truth.

When you study the Bible objectively, and by that I mean with *no theological grid guiding your interpretations and understanding,* you find that hell is the resulting punishment (or chastisement if you like), for disobedience, indifference, or laziness. No one is ever assigned to hell because he failed to believe *the right thing*, namely, some necessary doctrine listed by a Judeo-Christian teacher, preacher, or rabbi. *A person may go to hell because he had failed in the stewardships that God had delegated to him* even though he had believed in Jesus. It will be shocking to many to discover either presently or at his personal judgment that belief in Jesus is not a get-out-of-hell-free card.

There is nothing a person *can do* to get himself to heaven. There is nothing that a person *can believe* that will get himself to heaven. The Bible's message is simply not about finding NAR's road to heaven. Rejecting Jesus' claim to be the only path to heaven, a claim He never actually made, does not set aside God's plan for hell. It just opens the door for Christian participation!

## Missions Are no longer Necessary

The sixth doctrine that NAR is afraid will collapse, if the exclusivism of the gospel of Jesus Christ (i.e., that belief in Jesus is the only way to get to heaven) is proven wrong, is a proper motivation and rationale for evangelism and missions. It is quite telling for a person to tie hell to evangelism. Yes, I admit that I did this too for over thirty-five years of ministry. By tying hell to evangelism, all conservative, evangelical Christians are suggesting that *if there were no possibility of going to hell, there would be no reason for evangelism.*

NAR is not alone in thinking this way. I have had both pastors and seminary teachers assure me that such a result would naturally follow. They confirm the belief that if the world outside of Christendom can get to heaven without belief in Jesus Christ, then there is no reason for missions. And yet it is impossible to find in the Bible an approach to evangelism like we use today. Read through the NT. Does its "evangelism" focus upon saving people from hell?

If the point of evangelism were about saving people from hell and giving them the guarantee of a heavenly destiny, shouldn't we see sighs of relief from the apostle Paul on all of his missionary journeys when people either turned back to God[1] and/or believed in Jesus?[2] Shouldn't we see incidences of Paul giving praise to God for snatching souls from the fires of hell and delivering them into His presence forever?[3] Shouldn't we see Paul teaching others the correct message, which he carefully outlines for the rest of us, for getting people to heaven?

Evangelism and missions lack the man power and resources that are needed to reach the world because, quite frankly, most Christians really don't care enough for the people of other faiths to reach them for Christ, not even when their eternal destiny is at stake (as orthodox Christian teaching supposes). So how will a message like the one I'm suggesting change that? Won't the lack of interest and commitment to evangelism just grow worse?

It depends. What if Christians were told that they will be held accountable at the Judgment Seat of Christ for having reached the world with the message of Jesus? They may not care for the spiritual welfare of others to extend themselves to reach those of other faiths. But they may become slightly fearful of not doing it if they are convinced that they will be judged by Christ for not helping to accomplish this task in their life time. This is a stewardship that He had given them the time, talent, and treasure to perform. And

---

1 Acts 17:24-31; 26:18.

2 Acts 20:21.

3 The gaining and the saving described in 1Cor. 9:19-23 concerns the weak believer in Jesus, not the theologically doomed person.

He will require it of them as any master would require from any of his stewards a faithful management of their stewardships.

Think of the rich man and Lazarus. The only thing this man did to *deserve* hell, as far as we know from what Jesus revealed to us, was not using his resources to help Lazarus, the sick man at his door. In the same way, there will be consequences for all who have turned a deaf ear to those around them. Not to love others in word and deed is to live without the love of God and without the fear of God in our hearts.[1]

I think that warning is a much stronger motivation and rationale for participating in and furthering the missionary enterprise than what we usually hear from our pulpits. And, of course, there are other motivations and rationales for taking the Biblical message about Jesus to the world. But I already have your attention by the first one, don't I?

The summary of this chapter is very simple. Like in the movie, *The Princess Bride*, if Jesus never said it, it didn't happen. And if it didn't happen, there can be no consequences to denying that it happened. Buttercup wasn't married because she never said, "I do" to the priest's ceremonial question. Jesus isn't the only way to heaven because He never said that He was. And if Jesus never said that He was the only way to heaven, then all of NAR's fears are a product of men's imagination and are invalid altogether.

---

[1] 1John 2:15-17; 3:16-17; Heb. 10:31.

# Chapter 5

## Is It Just Semantics?

A recent conversation with a pastor in Dallas, Texas, on the issues touched upon in this and other books of late confirmed to me that the road ahead will be not only bumpy but also narrow. The difficulty? To convince others to take a fresh look at the terms that we have used to create the concepts that we have accepted as the meanings, or more precisely, as the referents within the message of the Bible.

Growing up in our American culture with a religious faith that has been handed down to us has its disadvantages as well as its advantages. The one that I confront most often is the firmly implanted conviction that there is nothing else to learn on the religious front. The truth has been handed down to us. All we need to do is accept it without hesitation or questioning. To quibble over the meaning of words is just a semantical misdirection designed to confuse and mislead the sheep. Doesn't 2Tim. 2:14-18 warn us about this very thing?

But as NAR has so correctly observed, we have come to different conclusions about the meaning of the message of the Bible because of our *cultural programming*. This is an outstanding observation. But like any other truth, we have been deceived into thinking it applies to others and not also to ourselves.

*What if* our Christian heritage is wrong?

*What if* the message of the Bible that we have accepted as true is found, upon closer examination, to be permeated by men's *assumptions that actually lack Biblical support*?

*What if* the message, that we learned and that we have taught to others, has been formulated very cogently and coherently into what appears on first encounter as a possible explanation of the truths of the Bible, but is, in the end, misleading?

*What if* that same message is actually responsible for some of the more unbecoming characteristics that have appeared in God's people? If the *assumptions* upon which the message is based are wrong, then it is very possible that the message itself might be wrong.

I am going to take a look at four terms, all of which NAR uses to defend its belief that faith in Jesus is the only way for a person to be forgiven and obtain a heavenly destiny. I hope to suggest a more Biblical understanding of those terms.

I will not be changing the essential meaning of the terms. As a result, all of the terms will have a familiar ring to them. But I will be demonstrating how the referents that we have attached to these terms are incorrect. For example, the Greek term for save (σωζω) will still mean to save, rescue, or deliver. The meaning of the term will not change. The issue will be *from what* is a person saved, rescued or delivered?

Again, the Greek term for justify (δικαιοω) will still mean to declare righteous rather than to make righteous. But the study will reveal that the Reformed concept of what is taking place when a person is justified is unsupportable, Biblically speaking. The term for being justified will still mean to declare righteous, but the issues will be *what is being declared righteous* and *what are the results of that declaration of righteousness*?

Furthermore, the Greek terms for eternal life (ζωη αιωνιος) will still refer to a life given by Jesus whenever a person believes in Him. But in this case the term *eternal* will be found to be wholly unsuited for understanding the message of the Bible. Rather than describing an endless duration, it will be very clear that the term refers to a long, indefinite period of time with a definite beginning and a definite ending. The Greek and Hebrew terms don't carry the same meaning that our English term does.

Also, the Greek term for kingdom (βασιλεια) is similar to the Greek phrase for eternal life. I may appear to be changing the meaning of the term completely because I refuse to allegorize or spiritualize the term as the Reformed tradition has done. The term kingdom usually brings to the mind of most readers a concept that necessarily includes a reigning king, ruling over a particular people group, in a land with borders and boundaries which define the sovereignty of the nation and the extent of the rule of its king. We will find that such an understanding is precisely the one the Scriptures present to its readers for the kingdom Jesus offered.

If we returned to the Biblical concepts of these four terms, we would have a much different theology than we do today. What follows is a summary that is based on a comprehensive study and detailed analysis of the terms involved. In fact, my goal is to make this summary as short as possible. But, I hope, it will be a convincing study, demonstrating the need to change our thinking about these terms and to receive the concepts that arise from a proper interpretation of them.

## Justification/Justify

The doctrine of justification, as almost everyone knows it today, *presupposes* the reality and truthfulness of several crucial concepts for the doctrine to be true. Don't underestimate the importance of these *assumptions*. They are as follows:

*Justification takes place at initial faith in God or at initial faith in Jesus* (if faith in Jesus had not been preceded by a faith in God). At this point an unbeliever *supposedly* becomes a

65

believer, a sinful person is forgiven, and a guilty person is declared to be in right standing with God forever.

*Justification removes the penalty from all the sins that a person will ever commit.* The punishment that a person deserves can never fall upon him because Jesus *supposedly* bore that punishment on the cross for him. Whenever a person is justified, the eternal penalties attached to his future sins are forgiven.

*Justification gives to the person believing the perfect righteousness of Jesus Christ* to stand before God in the judgment. With this righteousness, attributed to the defendant, God the Judge is *supposedly* able to pronounce an unchangeable acquittal from all charges laid against him for the rest of his life.

*Justification logically can occur only one time* (according to Berkhof). A person does not need to be forgiven of the same sins twice because God *supposedly* cannot condemn a person for a sin that He has already forgiven.

*This justification is logically demanded even though it cannot be explicitly identified (i.e., found) in the Scriptures* (according to Berkhof). Forensic justification is *assumed* to be included in (and the basis for) every "practical occurrence" of justification in a person's life. Whenever God justifies a person or his actions in daily life, it is only by previously granting to that person Christ's righteousness that practical righteousness can now flow from him. (In other words, this legal [or forensic] justification must be seen *everywhere* even though it has no *explicit* Biblical support *anywhere*.)

These are the important elements in the doctrine of justification. They were all clearly enumerated when the doctrine was finally revised and reformulated by the Reformers in the six-teenth and seventeenth centuries. Louis Berkhof in his *Systematic Theology* emphasizes the legal or forensic element as the thread that ties all the aspects of justification together. Consequently, without the legal aspect of justification, the foundation for this concept of justification is destroyed.[1]

I found it quite interesting, although it was after I had done my own research on justification, that Berkhof confesses that the Reformers *changed the meaning of justification from that found in the early church.* He believes that the early church was completely confused on the issue of justification. Consequently, it wasn't un-til the Reformation that a correct understanding of the doctrine was achieved.[2]

However, after completing my own independent study on justification, I've concluded that the early church was correct after all. When the Reformers changed the meaning (or referent) for justification, they actually distorted the Scriptural teaching of the doctrine. Since what is generally believed as the doctrine of justi-fication today is what has been handed down from the Reformers, the current, predominate understanding of this doctrine is op-posed to the belief of the early church, and can easily be seen to be contrary to the teaching of the Bible when it is interpreted lit-erally and without presuppositional, theological biases.

It actually is quite easy to arrive at a sound conclusion con-cerning the doctrine of justification. When one looks up every ref-erence to the terms for justification in the Bible, he will be at a loss when he doesn't find *any* of the elements required for the forensic concept of justification developed by the Reformers. As a result,

---

[1] L. Berkhof, *Systematic Theology.* Wm. B. Eerdmans Publishing Co., Grand Rapids, Michi-gan, 1941, pp. 510-26, but mainly, pp. 511-513, 517.
[2] Ibid.

in answer to each one of the points above, the following may be confidently said:

*There is no Scriptural example of a person being justified at his initial faith in God or at his initial faith in Jesus.*

The term justification is never used to describe a person's initial faith in God or the result of his initial faith in God. In fact, there is no example of initial faith in God to be found anywhere in the Bible. Consequently, it is sheer *conjecture* to believe that there is a justification of the kind that Berkhof logically needs for his Reformed theology to work. Can you give a verse that *explicitly* describes initial faith in God and designates that response as justification? I have found no such passage to illustrate, much less to defend, what I was taught about the moment that justification is supposed to occur.

*There is no passage that declares that at justification forgiveness of sins must be involved.*

Much less is it true that at justification *all one's sins,* including those in the future that the person has not committed yet, are removed (forgiven) along with the penalties resting upon them. Consequently, this principle relies upon nothing but *conjecture* as well. Can you give a passage that *explicitly* says that at *initial faith* (which, you will remember, can't be found in the Bible even once) all of a person's *future* sins are forgiven? There has to be a verse that *explicitly* says that in order for orthodox Christianity as formulated by the Reformers, and as presented in Nar, to be Biblical.

*There is no passage that explicitly says that Jesus' perfect righteousness is given to (or needed by) a person at his initial faith.*

This righteousness is, supposedly, needed to stand before God in order to receive God's acquittal from eternal condemnation. This concept, being without Scriptural support, is based upon *theological conjecture* alone. It was developed to support a preconceived theology rather than to reflect a clearly perceived teaching in the Bible.

We must keep all these thoughts together. We've already affirmed that there is no example of initial faith in God in the Bible that is referred to as an instance of justification.

We have also affirmed that forgiveness is not a necessary element of justification.

Now we are affirming that a perfect righteousness is *not given* to an individual, *nor* is it *needed* by him, when he is justified.

*Finally it is not true that justification only occurs one time.*

The accepted understanding of justification is that it can only occur one time since by it *all the penalties* resting upon *all the sins* a person will ever commit are forgiven altogether. A person can't be forgiven of the same sin twice nor can he be forgiven of the eternal penalty of confinement to hell only to have that penalty reapplied to him upon his next sin.

Yet we find that Abraham was declared to have been justified twice: once when he believed God's promise of a progeny,[1] and once when he offered up Isaac on the altar as a sacrifice to God.[2] *According to the apostle Paul, there is only one kind of justification. All justifications are to be exactly like Abraham's in Gen. 15:6.*[3] Essentially speaking, there is no other kind of justification. This is incredibly important to comprehend. When Abraham's background and the immediate context of Gen. 15 are carefully considered, it must be concluded that *there is no justification of the so-*

---

[1] Gen. 15:6.
[2] James 2:20-24.
[3] Rom. 4:22-24.

*called unbeliever which turns him into a believer.* Justification only happens to a person who is walking with God already just as Abraham had been from his first encounter with the living God (which encounter could have been in a vision or dream) during his days in Ur of the Chaldeans.[1]

If justification is not a once-for-all rap of God's judicial gavel declaring a person forgiven (of all sins, those in the past, those in the present, and those in the future) and righteous in His sight (because of the gift of righteousness given to him by Jesus Christ), then what is it?

It is exactly what Berkhof said the early church believed. Justification is God's declaration that a person and his response are righteous each time he responds in faith whenever he is attempting to obey God. *When God sees faith being exercised, He declares both the person and his response as righteous and pleasing in His sight.* God takes the faith being expressed *as* the righteousness needed to please Him. He is *not giving* the person righteousness as though it was some commodity to be given or received. He is declaring that the faith being expressed *is* the righteousness that He required in and from that person at that time.

Therefore, the apostle James got it right, and when the apostle Paul is properly understood, he agrees with James who said,

> "Was not Abraham our father *justified by works* when he offered Isaac his son on the altar?"

This particular Greek construction expects an affirmative answer to the question being asked. James expected all of his readers to answer the question, "Wasn't Abraham justified by works . . .?" with this response: "Yes, he was!"

Then James drew the logical, but every bit inspired conclusion

---

[1] Acts 7:2-4.

in verse twenty-four, saying,

"You see then that a man is *justified* by works and *not by faith alone.*"

This is a very clear presentation by James of what justification is. It is only because James doesn't agree with the Reformers' reformulation of the doctrine that it causes so much consternation.

Normally speaking then, justification includes both faith and obedience (i.e., works) unless the command that God gives to be obeyed is to do nothing but believe. Abraham didn't have the Law of Moses, which came over four hundred years later, to command him to do anything for the promise of a numerous progeny to be fulfilled in his life. Though there was no command of the Law to obey, obviously Abraham had to do something for the promise to be fulfilled and for him to have children. Since Sarah was still beautiful at ninety years old, he probably didn't need a lot of coercion to get him to do what was necessary. In the same way, most of God's commands require obedience for the promise to be fulfilled. The initial offer of the kingdom and the future offer of the kingdom are two very good examples of God requiring man's responsiveness (i.e., works of righteousness) in order for His promises to be fulfilled.

## Salvation/Save

The foundation for the concepts of salvation and of being saved is just as weak as the foundation for justification. Here are the principles that must be true for the orthodox, Christian position that NAR presents to be valid:

*Salvation occurs at initial faith in God or in Jesus.*

It is generally *assumed* that belief in God in the OT includes

71

a belief in the coming Messiah too. With this assumption, the obtainment of salvation is always connected to belief in Jesus.

*Salvation occurs by the sovereign grace of God through faith apart from works.*

No one can be saved if he does any work to aid in his salvation.

*Salvation results in the removal (i.e., forgiveness) of one's sins and the penalties resting upon them, including those which have not been committed yet.*

It is easy to see the assumed crossover between justification and salvation in this principle.

*Salvation results in the gift of eternal life.*

Eternal life is *assumed* to refer to an eternity with God in heaven. As a result, it is taught by some that if a person does not have an assurance of his salvation (or if he doesn't possess eternal security, which is the other side of the coin of salvation due to the way these doctrines are formulated), he can't actually have true salvation since these three concepts are all inseparably intertwined with one another.

*Salvation keeps a person from hell and guarantees him heaven for an eternal destiny.*

From this *assumed* premise, the doctrine of eternal security is usually developed. For most these last two principles will seem completely redundant.

While there are other principles we could deal with, these are the basic ones that seem to be the most talked about among Christians. Now we must ask, "Is this what salvation is?"

Let's critique each of these critical points about salvation and see where that critique leaves us.

*Does salvation occur at initial faith in God or in Jesus?*

No one can prove that when a person in the Bible first believes in Jesus that he had not believed in God before that. But if we use the examples of belief in Jesus in the Gospels, we see plainly that those who believed in Jesus had already believed in God the Father.[1] Consequently, salvation is not something that is offered to *a lost person doomed for hell* as the old paradigm of traditional Christianity presented by NAR firmly holds. Salvation is something that is being offered to a person who already believes in God but is in need of repentance and perseverance whenever entrance into the Messiah's kingdom is the topic of discussion.

*Does salvation take place by grace through faith apart from works?*

On rare occasions, yes! God can still work miraculously.[2] But at almost all other times the salvations that are needed cannot be achieved without works.[3] It really all depends upon which salvation one is discussing.

The salvation of Eph. 2:1-10 needs to be restudied with fresh eyes because the salvation that NAR presents, the one rescuing a person from entering into hell and delivering him instead to heaven for all eternity, is no longer a sound, interpretative option. That is to say, it cannot be found *explicitly* set forth in the Bible. *Salvation never means a deliverance from hell accompanied by an airlift to heaven.* If Eph. 2:1-10 does not refer to a salvation that is obtained apart from works, then to what does it refer? One really

---

[1] Cf., e.g., John 17:1-2, 6, 9.

[2] Both the salvation at the Red Sea (Ex. 14:13-14) and the salvation coming just before the Tribulation begins (1Thess. 5:9-10) are both examples of God's sovereign grace deliverances involving no specific works on man's part.

[3] Js. 2:14-17; Phil. 2:12-13.

good alternative to the traditional heaven-and-hell explanation can be easily offered as we allow the Scriptures to interpret themselves and to guide us into a better understanding.

Since part of the immediate context concerns being *delivered from personal sins*, the salvation that is mentioned in Eph. 2:5, 8 is probably of the same kind as the one the angel spoke about when he said to Joseph,

> "You shall call His name Jesus because He will *save His people from their sins*."[1] (Matt. 1:21)

Jesus came to save Israel from the hand of all who hate her. But that salvation had a condition: Israel had to repent and begin walking righteously before Jesus would fulfill the purpose for His first advent. Consequently, Jesus also came to be Israel's Savior from the personal sins that were disqualifying the nation for receiving the promised kingdom. This is a rescue, a salvation, from the ruination in this life caused by personal sins. After He and His disciples turned to the Gentiles, His intent was to save them in the same way for the same purpose.

The Ephesians were dead in their trespasses and sins, needing a Savior from them. They found what they needed in Jesus who supernaturally delivered them from the sins[2] that were enslaving them and from the ruination resulting from those sins. The things that they could not conquer alone, He conquered for them[3] by giving them a supernatural life[4] to address and overcome their sins.

Some sins are overcome miraculously and instantaneously.[5] Others are overcome as the result of works

---

[1] Notice that the verse does not say that Jesus would be a Savior, rescuing them from hell.

[2] Eph. 2:1-2.

[3] Rom. 8:37.

[4] Eph. 2:4-7.

[5] John 14:1, 27; 15:9, 11; Phil. 4:6-7.

completing the faith that God is expecting to be expressed,[1] and still others are overcome as a result of perseverance, that is, a persistent following of Jesus in faith.[2] Except for God's direct intervention, most *salvations* are equally dependent upon faith and works. The book of James clearly explains this salvation to us.[3] The dichotomies created by the old paradigm between grace and works and faith and works find little recognition, much less support, in the Scriptures.

*Does salvation involve the complete forgiveness of all sins a person will ever commit and the removal of all the penalties resting upon those sins?*

This principle is devised logically from the inherent theological needs created by the Reformed view of salvation. Since salvation is supposed to be a permanent and unchangeable right standing before God, forgiveness must include all the sins a person will ever commit. If it did not include them all, then whenever a person sins again, the penalty for that sin would, according to orthodox Christianity, send that person to hell even though he had previously received a pardon from hell relative to the forgiveness he had received over his former sins.

This theory of forgiveness is logical. It makes perfect sense. The problem with this theory is that there is no Biblical support for it. There is no Biblical teaching that *explicitly* says a person is forgiven of his future sins before he even commits them. But based upon the accepted belief system that NAR faithfully presents, such a forgiveness is inherently needed to support its understanding of salvation (and justification too). This is weighty proof that NAR's belief system is actually based upon *assumptions*

---

[1] This may have been the situation in Ephesus (Eph. 2:1-10). Cf., also Heb. 12:1, 4.
[2] Lk. 19:8-10. Cf., Lk. 9:23 also.
[3] Js. 2:14-17.

and *conjectures* rather than upon God's written revelation.

*Does salvation results in the gift of eternal life?*

That is a basic and central *assumption* of the arguments presented in NAR. Research here must begin at the definitional level. Exactly what is eternal life? When it is defined as going to heaven, or as a heavenly destiny, we remove ourselves from the teaching of the Bible and create our own definition in place of the true one. *Eternal life is not about eternity because there is no word in Hebrew or Greek that is equivalent to our English word eternal (or eternity).* The divine explanation of eternal life is *explicitly* given in John 17:3. Consequently, no understanding ought to be at variance with that revelation:

> *"And this is eternal life that they may know the only true God and Jesus Christ whom Thou has sent."*

This definition describes the eternal life that Jesus gave to His apostles, to His disciples, and to the greater multitude that trusted in Him as Messiah.[1] There is no mention of heaven or hell. No mention that forgiveness of sins is involved either. Eternal life is simply an abundant life[2] that is lived in fellowship with God[3] so that He can be personally known and experienced[4] in a way that could not take place without this resource of *life*.

*Does salvation keeps a person from hell and guarantees him a heavenly destination so that he can live with God forever?*

Shockingly, there is no Scriptural support for any of this. The interpreter must read these ideas into the text before he can get them from the text. Salvation is not about going to heaven. *There is nothing that a person can do to obtain that*

---

[1] John 20:31. Relate also John 17:2 to John 17:3.
[2] John 10:10b; Gal. 2:20.
[3] 1John 1:5-7.
[4] 1John 2:3-6; 3:5-6.

*destination; there is nothing that a person can believe that will secure that destination for him.* This is simply not the message of the Bible.

Because salvation is not what NAR thinks it is, it does not matter in the slightest whether a person is a Lordship salvationist or a Free Grace proponent. It does not matter that a person is a Calvinist or an Arminian. It does not matter if a person is a Catholic or a Protestant. God's grace, described in the Bible, won't get a person to heaven; man's works (nor God's works in and through the man) won't get him to heaven; faith, regardless of whether it comes from God or from man, won't get a person to heaven. There is absolutely nothing described in the Bible that has as its purpose getting a person to heaven. Because salvation is not about going to heaven, there is no road to heaven that can be found in the Scriptures. *The road to heaven is of man's own construction, not of God's revelation.*

## Eternal life

As I have already explained above, eternal life is not about heaven in any way, shape, or form. Eternal life is the term given to the extraordinary life that Jesus gives to the one who trusts in Him for it. In *the age to come* the life that a person is able to experience will be extraordinary. Jesus called it *the life of the age,* or eternal life because the term *eternal* was a reference to *this coming age* called the Davidic Kingdom of God's promised Messiah.

This life is nothing less than His own communicable life. Generally speaking, *He grants to the person who trusts in Him moment by moment the virtue, power, and wisdom that are inherent in His life.* Hence, to have Christ living within[1] is to have the Holy Spirit take

---

[1] Gal. 2:20.

what Jesus is offering[1] and give it to the trusting person[2] as he needs it. In this way, Christ can be said to be a person's life.[3] But to make eternal life a reference to heaven is to misunderstand and misuse the Biblical teaching of this phrase. The debate over whether eternal life emphasizes a quality of life or a duration of life misses the point. It is both. It is a quality of life that will exist for a specified duration upon planet earth.

## The Kingdom of Heaven/God

Probably the most significant Biblical discovery that a person can make is to come to a proper understanding of the kingdom of heaven (taken here as a synonym for the kingdom of God).[4] Confusion on this point will distort the Bible's message as few other mistakes can do.

NAR *assumes* that the kingdom of heaven is a synonym for salvation, for a heavenly destiny, and at times for God's work upon the earth presently. None of those *assumptions* can be proven *explicitly* from the Bible. The kingdom of heaven is the kingdom that God has promised to Israel in the OT.[5] But the expansion of the idea to include the Gentile nations is also present in the OT.[6] So, the kingdom is a physical kingdom, upon this present earth,[7] with the promised Messiah ruling over not only Israel's individual kingdom but over all of the kingdoms in the whole world at the same time.[8] Satan, knowing the ultimate goal

---

[1] John 16:12-15.

[2] Eph. 3:16-17; Gal. 2:20. Cf., also John 10:27 and John 20:31.

[3] Col. 3:4.

[4] E.g., in Matt. 19:23-24 they are used interchangeably.

[5] Cf., 2Sam. 7:16 with Lk. 1:32-33; Isa. 9:7; 11:1-16.

[6] Cf., Isa. 2:2-4. This harmonizes with Matt. 25:34.

[7] Dan. 7:27.

[8] Ps. 2:1-12. Cf., also Matt. 4:8-9.

of Jesus' coming to earth in His first advent, therefore, offered Him all the kingdoms of the world if He would worship him.

The offer of the kingdom is not, therefore, an offer of an eternity with God in the heavens. Neither is it an offer of an escape from hell. Nor is it a synonym for salvation which is usually defined in terms of heaven or hell. And it certainly is not a general description of the work of God presently upon the earth.

This kingdom is future.[1] It is impossible for it to have been inaugurated already, waiting for its full display at some point in the future. Those ideas are more theological creations by men who refuse to take all the teachings of the Bible on the kingdom into their formulations. As I have said earlier, it is easy to make the Bible say a lot of different things when it is not interpreted literally and taken as a whole. But, generally speaking, *it is a commitment to preconceived theological ideas flowing from well-developed systematic theologies that keep most people from most of the truths of the Bible.* The subject of the kingdom has been more thoroughly covered in my previous works.[2]

The point that the reader should notice is that none of the usual suspects ~ justification, salvation, eternal life, and the kingdom of heaven ~ teach what NAR has concluded that they teach. They don't even broach the subject of going to heaven or of having an escape from hell. Consequently, to use any of these terms in an attempt to prove that Christianity provides the only pathway to heaven is fruitless. They simply don't address the subject at all. Keep that in mind as we move into NAR's main points in defense of the *supposed* exclusivity of belief in Jesus as the only way to heaven.

---

[1] Lk. 19:11-12.
[2] See *The Prodigal Paradigm* for an extended discussion.

The need to bounce back and forth between these topics is caused by the fact that none of them teach all that is needed to support the exclusivity of Christianity. It will become obvious, I hope, that taking all of these topics together won't provide all that is needed to establish this doctrine of exclusivity either.

# Chapter 6

## Our Religious Sub-Culture Misleads us

I was so glad to see NAR's focus, momentary though it was, on the impact of each person's culture upon his understanding of the Bible. NAR stated so wonderfully this warning in answer to its question: Why do not all Christians come to the same conclusions when they study the Bible? Its answer to its own question was:

> "The limitations of human understanding, *the impact of culture, and the influence of our particular faith tradition* or personal experiences all shape our interpretation of Scripture, whether we are willing to admit it or not."[1] (emphases mine)

I would like to apply NAR's observation to the belief in Christianity's exclusivism. What would we think if we were to discover that this exclusivism, that NAR tries to defend, first developed from a sub-culture outside the guidelines of the Bible?[2] Is this doctrine a creation of a religious sub-culture of Christianity? Is any individual Christian naturally immune to the influence of this sub-culture? How is anyone supposed to establish (or reject) the validity of NAR's claim that belief in Jesus is the exclusive way, the one-and-only means, of getting to heaven? If the Bible doesn't *explicitly* say it, does anyone have the right to infer it?

---

[1] Ibid, p. 40.

[2] Cf., N.T. Wright, *Surprised by Hope*, rethinking heaven, the resurrection, and the mission of the church, Harper One, 2008, who argues that God's plan is not to save man from the earth to heaven, but to use man to save the earth for God's ultimate display of Himself and His will. Bringing heaven to earth and not man to heaven is the message of the Bible according to Wright. Hence, the whole idea of salvation that is typically taught within Christendom is backwards and needs to be rethought.

The apostle Paul described in his letter to the Corinthians the power that culture has when he said,

> "However, not all men have this knowledge [the truths that he had mentioned in vv. 1-6]; but some, *being accustomed to* the idol until now, eat food *as if* it were sacrificed to an idol; and their conscience being weak is defiled." (1Cor. 8:7, emphases mine)

Paul was basically saying that a person's conscience, molded and trained by his own culture, including his *religious culture*, which was the primary cultural aspect that Paul was referring to in this passage, is able to overturn or reject God's revelation when he hears it. If we didn't have an infallible, inerrant guide from God, that would be a frightening thought. There would be, at best, only a very difficult way back to the truth of God apart from His continuing revelations, both from the Scriptures and from creation, to all men.

Let me show you the reason that a proper understanding of our religious sub-culture is so sobering. What Paul would say to every single person is this: Are you a Baptist? Your Baptist culture may prevent you from receiving the word of God that is being presented to you. Are you a Presbyterian? Your Presbyterian culture may be keeping you from truth that God has revealed. Are you a Methodist? Your Methodist culture may be preventing you from understanding some things that could be life changing. And on we could go until we cover all the denominations within Protestantism. Catholicism, as well as every other religion in the world, must be alerted to the same apostolic warning: *your faith (that is, your religious belief system) may be keeping you from God's truth.* Follow the crowd if you will, but know that such a decision may be to your own detriment. Your religious circumstances can keep you from the truth that you need to receive from God.

Of course, we usually only think in terms of the world and its ideas when we think of hindrances to our faith. But Paul wanted us to understand that every aspect of our own culture can be bombarding our minds and consciences with suggestions that produce a skewed standard, entirely removed from God's truth. *Have our own religious cultures misread the Bible?* Have they drawn conclusions that are actually inconsistent with the Bible's full teaching? The *supposed* exclusivity of the gospel of Christ maybe just such an issue.

As long as you remain a pawn in the chess game of religious convictions, you will never know for sure. You may think you know for sure because you have such implicit trust in your pastor or teacher or elder or bishop. But since he can be wrong,[1] and since the majority can be wrong,[2] God gave us an infallible, inerrant canon of truth for each of us to use in critiquing those who teach us.[3] It is very clear from the apostle Paul that differences of opinion on doctrinal issues may be present,[4] but should not divide us.[5]

What if *our religious culture* has hijacked the Biblical concept of salvation and put another view in its place? Or to put this more pointedly, if NAR has misunderstood the Biblical concept of salvation, and has trained its readers in that misunderstanding so that all that is taught on this subject is decidedly out of step with the message of the Bible, then none of its arguments, regardless of their apparent cogency and coherence, will be helpful in the slightest degree. The message of NAR would be an example of

---

[1] Cf., 1Thess. 5:19-22.

[2] We should have learned this lesson from the spies that searched out the land of Canaan or from Jeremiah standing alone rebuking the entire nation of Israel.

[3] Cf., Deut. 13:1-4; and relate Matt. 5:17-19 to Matt. 7:13-27.

[4] Phil. 3:15-16.

[5] 1Thess. 5:19-22. Cf., also, 1Cor. 1:10-13; John 17:22-26. See also Tit. 3:9-11.

history repeating itself.[1] We are all on a spiritual journey. God expects us all to be faithful to Him rather than to any other religious authority. We do that by bringing every one of our thoughts captive to the obedience[2] that Christ has set before us in His Word to us.[3]

Whenever we preach *assumptions*, even when we don't realize that we are doing it, we are in a bad place. NAR has done this in regard to salvation being a reference to a heavenly destination. Such a *faux pas* is so easy to make that it is difficult to find expositions on the Bible without such *assumptive* reasoning.

NAR offers an example of such *assumptive* exposition when it deals with Adam and Eve in Genesis two and three.

NAR *assumes* that the issue between God and mankind's first parents concerns their salvation even though no reference is made to salvation in the context.

NAR *assumes* that they were trying to find another way to be saved other than believing on Jesus for salvation even though no such option was given to them in the context. The prophecy of an off-spring of Eve who would crush the head of the serpent was totally misunderstood by Adam and Eve as far as we can tell from the context. In addition, the prophecy comes *after* their restoration to communion and fellowship with God.

NAR *assumes* that God had trained Adam and Eve in the Christian theology that it is propagating many millennia later.

All of these *assumptions* are groundless.

NAR *assumes* that, when the leaves that Adam and Eve had covered themselves with were replaced by the skins of slain animals, in this covering replacement God is explaining the need for

---

[1] Jer. 23:31-32.
[2] 2Cor. 10:5; 1Thess. 5:19-22.
[3] 2Tim. 3:16-17.

a blood sacrifice to cover their sins. Not only is there no hint of such a transaction taking place in Genesis two and three, there are *explicit* statements in the Scriptures that explain the reasons that such a thing could not have taken place.

There are at least two Biblical reasons that NAR's suggestion is an impossible view of Adam's and Eve's situation. 1.) Sacrifices prescribed by the Law God gave through Moses only covered *un-intentional* sins.[1] There were no sacrifices which could remove the sin, the guilt, or the resulting barrier between God and man for premeditated sins. 2.) The sacrifice for sins unintentionally committed was completely burned outside the camp, skins and all. If God had killed an animal for a blood sacrifice for sin, the skins of that sacrifice would not be available for clothing since they would have been burned on the altar with the rest of the animal.[2] For these two reasons it is impossible to support the idea that God was providing a sin sacrifice to clothe Adam and Eve after their sin. NAR's *assumption* simply does not fit the revelation that God has given to us.

Another *assumption* that NAR is counting on is that God has *one prescribed way* to obtain forgiveness of sins.[3] This prescribed way of obtaining forgiveness of sins is, of course, by believing in Jesus Christ for that forgiveness. That view of forgiveness has been the dominate belief created by the religious sub-culture of Christianity for at least the last five hundred years.

But the longevity of a belief doesn't make it true. So, the reader must answer the question, "What are the means for obtaining forgiveness that the Bible *explicitly* describes?" How many can you actually list? Yes, there are more than one means of attaining

---

[1] Num. 15:22-31.
[2] Lev. 4:1-12, esp. v. 11.
[3] NAR, p. 27.

forgiveness of sins *explicitly* outlined in the Scriptures. Has your particular Christian sub-culture limited you to believe that there is only one?

But my point here is to draw attention to the *assumptive* rationale that undergirds the entirety of NAR on the subject of salvation. In the case of forgiveness, *belief in Jesus isn't one of the means of obtaining forgiveness for all of the sins a person has committed!* And yet, belief in Jesus is the only means that most Christians have ever been taught for obtaining forgiveness of sins. That creates quite a dilemma. Can you recall a verse that says, "Believe on the Lord Jesus Christ, and you shall be forgiven of all of your sins (past, present, and future)?" On the other hand, maybe you can recall verses that offer (or grant) forgiveness without any requirement to believe in Jesus. How do you harmonize such verses with the restrictive theology presented by NAR?

As NAR points out, Satan has long been considered the great deceiver. Part of his plan of deception is to mislead some to offer an alternative way to God. Without trying to be dramatic or shocking, I want to suggest that *this is exactly what orthodox Christianity is doing; it is offering an alternative path to God.* The way to God has long been open, and all men have had access to it because Jesus died to provide it for everyone.

The access to God not only provides a way back into God's presence, but it also provides a full and complete forgiveness whenever that access, or path if you prefer, is used. *This access is available without believing in Jesus* (as several of the means[1] to obtain forgiveness demonstrate). Consequently, for anyone to require all men to believe in Jesus in order to return to God and

---

[1] So far, by my count, there are eleven different means for obtaining forgiveness of sins *explicitly* revealed in the Bible. How many of those can you name? Remember: believing in Jesus is NOT one of them.

have forgiveness of sins is to create *a new way* back to God, one that is not available to all men.

As NAR continues expounding its own ingrained religious sub-culture, it gives four examples of Satan's "servants of righteousness":[1]

Joseph Smith, the founder of Mormonism

Muhammad, the founder of Islam

Any religious leader that says that *faith in Christ is not sufficient to obtain the forgiveness of sins.*

Evangelical pastors who preach that *sincere followers of other faiths will be welcomed into God's presence.*

The last two of NAR's examples are of particular interest because they have obvious connections to the *supposed* exclusivity of belief in Jesus as the only way to God (i.e., the only means of getting to heaven).

From the Scriptures alone, how would you answer the question, "Is faith in Jesus sufficient to obtain forgiveness of sins?" The forgiveness that we are talking about is one that deals with *all of the sins a person has ever committed and will ever commit.* The reader should recall the previous discussion on this topic. It does no good to have a forgiveness for one sin but not for all the others that have been or will be committed. Does Jesus ever invite a person to believe in Him to receive such a comprehensive forgiveness?

Also, from the Scriptures alone, how would you answer the question, "Can sincere followers of other faiths *be welcomed* (or approved) by God?" NAR *assumes* that being welcomed or approved to God is the same thing as being saved. Does the Bible

---

[1] Jeffress, pp. 28-29.

bear that *assumption* out? Or does it make it very clear that being welcomed by God and being saved are two very different things altogether? This is no small matter. It will determine how we see the rest of the world and the attitude we take in addressing all the peoples from different cultures and from different religious beliefs.

> *What if* the rest of the world isn't nearly as separated from God as Christianity claims it is?
>
> *What if* many throughout the world are already acceptable to God (or welcomed by Him) even though they have not believed in Jesus?

These are not simply hypothetical questions. These are actually the evaluations given in the Scriptures as we will see later on. *The good news of the Bible is actually a whole lot better than the good news that has been accepted among Christians as their gospel of grace.*

It is the task of this book to expose this exclusivity of belief in Jesus Christ as the only way to heaven to the light of theology-free investigation, and to the just criticism that it deserves. *Our orthodox Christian sub-culture has changed the message of the Bible.* We must turn back to the Bible if we want to reach an ever-shrinking world.[1]

---

[1] See my book, *A Shrinking World Requires a Better Christianity.*

# Chapter 7

# What Exactly Did Jesus Claim? Pt. 1

When NAR summarizes Jesus' claims, it believes it has a solid foundation for its doctrine of exclusivity. Using classic passages, NAR offers some of the best that Christianity has as proof that Jesus required a person to believe in Him as the only way to get to heaven. Since Jesus' Sermon on the Mount is so key for NAR's arguments, we will begin our investigation with it. In doing so, I would ask the reader to carefully observe what the passage *actually* says in contradistinction to what NAR *infers from it*. Matthew chapters five through seven set forth this one sermon of Jesus'.

## Matt. 7:13-14: The only way to Heaven

NAR uses Matt. 7:13-14, which is probably the most often quoted passage of Scripture in this book, to show how Jesus *supposedly* "slammed the door on the idea that *all religious paths* ultimately lead to *eternal life*."[1] Matt. 7:13-14 say,

> "***Enter*** through the narrow gate; for ***the gate*** is wide ***and the way*** is broad that leads to ***destruction,*** and there are many who enter through it. For ***the gate*** is small ***and the way*** is narrow that leads to ***life,*** and there are few who find it." (Matt. 7:13-14, emphases mine).

The reader ought to easily observe NAR's *modus operandi* here, and understand that its approach really never varies throughout the book. *NAR's M.O. is to assume the equivalence of various terms throughout the book even though those terms are never said to be*

---

[1] NAR, p. 25.

*equivalent in the Bible.* This is not unique to NAR; it is the necessary approach by all who use the theology developed within the subculture of orthodox Christianity as their template for understanding the Scriptures. No one term supplies all the necessary facts that are needed to establish the doctrine of exclusivity sufficiently. The question then arises is, Can all the terms taken together and handled as though they all addressed the doctrine of exclusivity establish the belief incontrovertibly? This obvious lack of conclusive evidence should motivate each person must do his own word studies in order for him to test what others are telling him.

Because the evidence is inadequate, a lot of assumptions need to be made in order to give the appearance that the Bible teaches what it never explicitly says. Some of NAR's assumptions can be listed as follows:

> NAR *assumes* that in Matt. 7:13-14 Jesus is talking about *entering heaven.*
> It *assumes* that the *destruction* mentioned here is a reference to *hell.*
> It *assumes* that *life* is a reference to eternal life which is generally defined by NAR as a life with God for all eternity. *Eternal life in NAR is just another way, usually, of referring to heaven.*
> It *assumes* that Jesus' little analogy of the two gates and the two ways is a portrayal of *salvation* which is an explanation of how a person gets to heaven.
> It *assumes* that entering either one of the gates is a once-for-all decision that automatically leads down a path to the destination that is described.

Such *assumptions,* as NAR makes here, are absolutely necessary. How else could this passage be a salvation analogy, necessarily describing a grace-through-faith-apart-from-works phenomenon if the gates, along with their connecting paths, were not one-time responses?

NAR also *assumes* that the *saved* and the *lost* are opposite peoples. These two designations are typically used theologically rather than Biblically. As one studies the Bible, however, he finds that the saved can still be lost (contrary to the accepted theological scheme), and the lost may not need to be saved (in the sense that is commonly employed within Christianity's sub-culture) for them to be acceptable to God.

For example, one writer, Dr. Robert N. Wilkin, makes a case for the view that in the Bible only the saved are able to be lost.[1] Obviously, if there is any truth to that statement, then both words, *saved* and *lost*, need to be reevaluated. If NAR's interpretation is true, the *saved* can't also be the *lost*. But Wilkin has shown that such is simply not the case.

> When you read Matt. 7:13-14, do you see heaven mentioned?
> Do you see hell mentioned?
> Do you see a reference to a salvation from hell?
> Do you see any hint of something, anything, being offered as a free gift to the person who wants to enter the narrow gate? In fact, do you see any mention that faith is required but that it must function apart from works?

NAR *assumes* that the passage addresses *all of these things* when, in fact, it doesn't mention *any of them.*

What exactly was it that Jesus was commanding His audience, filled as it was with His disciples who had already believed in Him as Messiah, to enter? In Matt. 5:20 and Matt. 7:21 a clear answer can be found.

> "For I say to you that unless your *righteousness* exceeds that of the Scribes and Pharisees, you will by no means (or, certainly not) *enter the kingdom of heaven.*" (Matt. 5:20, emphases mine)
>
> "Not all who say to Me, 'Lord, Lord,' will *enter the kingdom of*

---

[1] See his book, *The Ten Most Misunderstood Words in the Bible.*

*heaven* but the one who *does the will of My Father* who is in heaven." (Matt. 7:21, emphases mine)

From just these two verses alone, it is clear that Jesus is talking about entering the kingdom of heaven. To enter that kingdom one needs *practical* righteousness, not the *imputed* righteousness that is *assumed* to be given as a free gift to the person who believes in Jesus. No such righteousness is ever *explicitly* said to be given for the purpose of qualifying a person to be pardoned or of guaranteeing to him an eternal destiny in heaven.

*Even if there were an imputed righteousness to be obtained, it is not the kind of righteousness that grants a person entrance into the kingdom of heaven.* If it were, Jesus would not be commanding His apostles to keep on pursuing additional righteousness for entering the kingdom.[1] They had already believed in Jesus and, in NAR's perspective, would have been given this free gift of righteousness at the moment they first believed. With this gift of righteousness, it is *supposed* by NAR's theology, they had all they needed to be rightly related to God, to enter the kingdom, and to be assured of a heavenly destiny when they died.

But now over a year later, Jesus is commanding them to seek another kind of righteousness altogether. They need another kind of righteousness, one that is different from Christ's righteousness which is imagined to be imputed (i.e., given as a free gift like some commodity) to the one who believes in Jesus. Only this other kind of righteousness will admit them into the kingdom of heaven. So, Jesus said to them,

> "But *be seeking first the Kingdom of God and His righteousness* and all these things will be added to you." (Matt. 6:33, author's translation emphasizing the present imperative)

---

[1] Matt. 6:33.

The issue throughout the entirety of Jesus' sermon is a kingdom issue with *supposedly* saved people, the apostles,[1] *standing with the multitudes of other listeners outside of the kingdom[2] seeking entrance.*[3] Consequently, when Jesus said, "Enter," in Matt. 7:13, He was speaking of entering the kingdom of heaven which cannot refer to salvation because, according to NAR's theology, the apostles were already saved, having believed in Jesus earlier in His ministry. Nor is it possible that the kingdom of heaven could refer to heaven since this kingdom must come out of heaven to earth[4] to be established upon this earth.[5]

Nowhere in this text is Jesus describing two roads, one leading to heaven and the other leading to hell. *That conclusion is NAR's theology talking which is quite contrary to the point that Matthew, the original author of this passage, was making.*

The typical way most evangelical expositors try to harmonize these concepts is by assuming that Jesus is preaching to a mixed multitude, that is, to a crowd that is made up of both *believers* and *unbelievers*. Hence, whenever the need arises, the expositor can flip back and forth between these two groups. If the statement doesn't seem to fit a description of a believer, then the unbeliever is called up to take the brunt of that warning. But if the statement is some blessing or a promise of some future blessing, it obviously must be addressed to the believers in the crowd so they become the recipients of those blessings.

---

[1] Matt. 5:1-2ff; Lk. 6:12-49. I am calling the apostles saved in accordance with NAR's theology (mostly based upon Acts 16:30-31 which will be discussed later). But if you look up save/saved/salvation in your concordance, you will find that *the apostles were never described as saved*. What Biblical conclusions can you draw from that fact?
[2] Matt. 5:20.
[3] Matt. 7:21.
[4] Matt. 6:10.
[5] Dan. 7:27.

The biggest problem with this flip-flop exegesis is that Matthew is consistent all the way through his record of Jesus' sermon in identifying *all of the addressees of Jesus' message* as those who have a relationship with the one true God in a Father-son fashion. Sixteen times Matthew describes Jesus' entire audience as having a heavenly Father, the same One that Jesus teaches them all to pray to. The flip-flop exegetical method of attempting to understand Jesus' sermon reveals the theology of the commentator rather than the thinking of the Christ giving the sermon. Whenever an expositor tries to force a passage to fit into a theological paradigm or template that it can't naturally fit into, glaring discrepancies usually arise as they do here. Clearly Matt. 7:13-14 have been taken out of their context and made to support the theology espoused in NAR.

## Road to Destruction?

Did Jesus give any clues for properly identifying the *destruction* to which the wide gate and the broad path lead? NAR *assumes* that the destruction is a reference to hell. Unfortunately, so does Zane Hodges in his Greek English interlinear (see footnote below).[1] But when we realize that this command was addressed to the apostles of Jesus as well as to the whole multitude, a reference

---

[1] I found it disappointing that Zane Hodges, et al, gave the following word study on p. 22 of *The NKJV Greek English Interlinear New Testament* (published by Thomas Nelson Publishers, Nashville, 1994): απωλεια: Noun that can mean waste (Matt. 26:8), but in the NT is nearly always personal, meaning destruction, ruin, perdition. Once (Acts 25:16, NU omits) it means physical death, but elsewhere spiritual death, *eternal destruction*. Derived from perish, be ruined, be destroyed, be lost, the noun απωλεια appears to focus on the *utter loss or ruin as a 'final destiny' for the wicked* (as here in Matt. 7:13; also Rev. 17:8). A 'son of perdition' (John 17:12; 2Thess. 2:3) is one so destined." I have not found those phrases that I have boldfaced above anywhere *demanded* in the Bible. Neither the noun nor the verb describes anything beyond the wasteful ruination of earthly life which sometimes ends in a person's physical death.

to hell seems hardly legitimate unless NAR's teaching on salvation and eternal security are also called into question.

If the term *destruction* was a reference to hell, then even the apostles, who were mainly the ones being addressed by Jesus, can still choose to take the wide gate and the broad path and end up in hell. But the term actually refers to a perdition or ruin in the sense of destroying one's earthly life.[1] It should be remembered that Jesus later in His ministry warned all the apostles that such a path was possible for all of them to take. Even though he did not take the wide gate and the broad path,[2] Judas did end up as *a son of perdition* (or destruction),[3] and possibly as the epitome of such a person. Nevertheless, there is overwhelming evidence that Judas had believed in Jesus and had faithfully followed Him, obtaining as a consequence of his service to Jesus a rulership within the coming kingdom.

As a result, it does not matter whether a person ends up *ruining* his life by taking a long journey toward that end through the wide gate and upon the broad path or by one brief, misguided, and entangling episode in his life, the ruin is still the same even though the consequences may be radically different. Never is the noun perdition (or destruction) used as a reference to hell unless the use of it in Rev. 17:8, describing the demise and immediate destiny of the Beast, is the one exception.

The fact is the context of Jesus' entire sermon, taking up three entire chapters, is not about heaven or hell. Heaven is not being

---

[1] Cf., Matt. 16:24-27 where Jesus commands the apostles not to *destroy* their lives (the Greek term used here, απολλυμι, is the one from which *destruction* is derived!). It is usually translated *to lose* in Matt. 16:25-27. Jesus assured Judas of a very different destiny from the one Hodges describes (Lk. 22:28-30). For more on this see my book, *Judas and Divine Grace.*

[2] Lk. 22:28-30.

[3] John 17:12.

sought; hell is not trying to be avoided. As a result, the *destruction* in Matt. 7:13 cannot be a reference to hell. To make the destruction mentioned here a reference to hell is to read into the passage what is never brought up in a sermon three chapters long. That is a classic example of eisegesis, reading into a text what isn't there.

## Road to Life?

Did Jesus give any clues for properly identifying the *life* that He mentioned to which the narrow gate and difficult path lead? This reference to *life* cannot refer to an eternal destiny gained by grace through faith apart from works. The context of Jesus' whole sermon requires grace and faith and works, all working together. Consequently, if *life* were a reference to heaven or to the traditional, Christian understanding of salvation, then it is an inescapable fact that works are needed to obtain it. But since neither heaven nor hell are mentioned anywhere in the sermon as destinations to be sought, it would be pure conjecture to read heaven into the sermon at this point.

The *life* that Jesus is referring to is something that is still future. But importantly, it is something that requires works to finally obtain. Jesus' sermon is about what it takes to enter the kingdom of heaven. To enter one must go through a narrow gate and travel down a difficult path in order to arrive at the door to the kingdom. *That earthly kingdom of Messiah is here called life.* This is easily proven when it is remembered that *Jesus' whole sermon was about entering the Kingdom*[1] that He was offering in fulfillment of OT covenants and promises. But that entrance could be gained only by those whose lives qualified them for kingdom participation. Their lives had to be judged by God as being righteous. This

---

[1] Matt. 5:20. This is usually taken to be the theme verse for the whole sermon.

judgment or evaluation by God is called His justification. Consequently, Jesus commanded His whole audience to seek the righteous lifestyle[1] that He had outlined for them in the Law and the Prophets. That lifestyle would qualify them for entrance.[2]

There is no reference to heaven here. There is no salvation offered here. There is no exclusive path to heaven outlined here. All such ideas seep into the passage from the theology of the interpreter, a theology that hides the true teachings of Jesus.

One last thought on Matt. 7:13-14 that reveals how much at odds a proper interpretation of this passage is with the concept of salvation propagated by NAR's theology. It should not escape your notice that both *gates* have a *pathway* upon which one is expected to travel. *One path leads to life; the other path leads to destruction.* Hence, it is not the gate alone that describes either option. It is a gate *and* a path that constitute each option.

## Both Gates Require Works to Follow

Now to point out the obvious: if a path needs to be followed in order to arrive at a destination, then the journey that is being described involves works. *Every walk, every pathway, involves steps which is another way of saying works.* If the narrow gate and the difficult (or constricted or confined) path describe salvation, then it is obvious that *a great deal of effort, that is, a great deal of work involving a lot of steps*, is involved in obtaining the salvation that Jesus is talking about here. Consequently, this salvation cannot be the same as the salvation that is *supposedly* obtained by grace through faith *apart from works* according to the traditional interpretation of

---

[1] Matt. 6:33. This righteousness is the result of obeying Jesus' instructions given in this sermon (Matt. 7:24-27; cf., Lk. 6:46-49).

[2] If Jesus' command in Matt. 7:13 (Enter!) is related back to Matt. 5:20, He intent is clear.

Eph. 2:8-9. It will become rather apparent that these two passages are not describing the same thing.[1]

This passage says none of the things that NAR wants it to say. It has to *assume* that the things that are mentioned refer to a salvation from hell and a guarantee of heaven. But heaven and hell aren't mentioned even once! NAR is followed by most other Christian expositors regardless of their denominational affiliation. Why? Because the interpretation that NAR gives here conforms to the accepted theology that must be found in every passage. *What is found here in this passage is what is needed to be found for the teaching to be considered orthodox Christianity.* But it is obvious that there is great disparity between what this passage actually says and the orthodox Christian teaching on salvation. When we allow our theology to guide our exegesis, we will only get the message of our past theologians rather than the message which is from God.

### John 14:6: Jesus, the only way to the Father

NAR turns to John 14:6 in an attempt to establish its supposition that Jesus clearly taught that *belief in Him* is the only way to heaven. Obviously, if Jesus taught this idea, it is an absolute, permitting no deviation. So clear is this claim in NAR that it calls Jesus the *gatekeeper to heaven*. It concludes,

> "No one gets there [i.e., heaven] without coming **through** Him [i.e., Jesus]."[2] (brackets and emphasis mine)

Jesus might be the gate keeper of heaven. If He is, He is that not

---

[1] For the same reason, it seems impossible to make either Acts 11:14, Cornelius' salvation, or Acts 16:30-31, the Philippian jailer's salvation, the same salvation that we read about in Eph. 2:1-10. Both of those salvations are *future*; the one in Ephesians is *past*.
[2] NAR, p. 98.

because He ever claimed that *faith in Him* was the only way to get there.

NAR recognizes that there are two issues in play in John 14:6: a *where* question and a *how* question. The *where* issue focuses upon the destination. The *how* issue focuses upon the means or the way that leads to this destination. While NAR doesn't deal with the where issue right away, it does explain that Jesus will answer that question when He *ascends into heaven* in plain view of all His disciples (Acts 1:9-11).[1] Hence, by ascending into heaven, Jesus *supposedly* designates the destination He had in mind. But NAR's understanding is only a half-truth which changes the focus and emphasis of Jesus' comments. How does one correct this? Is there more to the passage than NAR has addressed?

First, Jesus specifically identified the *where*, that is to say His destination, when He gave His original statement. He said,

"... In My Father's house there are many dwelling places... *I am going to the Father* ..."[2] (emphasis mine)

How could Jesus make His destination any clearer than that? Jesus is not going *to heaven*; He is going back *to the Father* who happens to be in heaven. If the Father had been in any other place than heaven at this time, then Jesus would have gone there to be with the Father. Jesus is going to a person, not to a place.

Jesus' apostles did not understand what He was talking about any better than the Jews had who were opposing Him earlier in His ministry.[3] Since Jesus said the same thing to His apostles who believed in Him as He had said to the Jewish leaders who didn't believe in Him, we have our first clue that *going to the Father* is not

---

[1] Ibid.
[2] Cf., John 14:2, 12, 28; 16:5.
[3] John 8:21-27.

a matter of having faith in Jesus. *Going to the Father* was a matter of fulfilling God's divinely appointed plan to bring each person before Him to render a judgment upon his life.[1] Each person has a time set for him to go to the Father the way Jesus was going to Him, namely, by physically dying.

In John 14:10 and following, there is more information about the Father than in any other single passage in the NT. Jesus, having accomplished all the work that the Father had sent Him to do, was headed back to the Father's house in the third heaven[2] to wait for His time to return[3] back to earth to reign over the kingdom[4] that He had been offering to the Jews throughout His ministry. The focus of Jesus' comments is upon a return to the relationship, or fellowship, with the Father that He had before His incarnation.[5]

When Jesus told Peter and the other apostles that they could not go where He was going, was He implying that they had some spiritual need that had to be met before they would be ready to go to the Father in heaven? That is how most Christians use the verse in their evangelistic tracts and messages.

Typically, the evangelist says, "You must believe in Jesus in order to go to heaven because the Bible says, 'No one can come to the Father except through Jesus.'" But that use of the verse doesn't exactly ring true, does it? Jesus gave His great "I am" statement to those who had already believed in Him. After all, He was addressing His eleven apostles in the upper room when He gave it. Consequently, John 14:6 was not an invitation to anyone to begin believing in Jesus so that he could go to heaven when he died.[6]

---

[1] Heb. 9:27.
[2] Cf., 2Cor. 12:1-2 and relate it to Rev. 21:1-2, 10.
[3] Lk. 19:11-27; Acts 3:11-26.
[4] Ps. 110:1; Ps. 2:1-12.
[5] John 1:1-2. Cf., also Jesus' high priestly prayer in John 17.
[6] John 17:6-9.

Jesus had already explained to the apostles the reason they couldn't go with Him to the Father.[1] He basically told them that it was *not their time to die physically*! That was the reason they couldn't go with Him presently. But they would go later on in their lives.

Jesus couldn't die before His time to die by crucifixion had arrived even though some wanted to stone Him to death[2] and others wanted to kill Him by throwing Him off a cliff.[3] His death could not come before His appointed time to die had come.[4] In the same way, the apostles could not go to the Father with Jesus because their time to die physically had not yet come.

Jesus was comparing the way *He* was going to the Father *at present* with the way *they* would be able to go to the Father *at present*. No one, who was hearing Jesus' words at the moment they were given, would have understood them the way NAR has interpreted them. He was not giving *an evangelistic formula*. He had already assured them all that they would be with Him in the Father's house eventually.[5] *He was giving them assurance that, while they could not go **with Him** to the Father, they could go **through Him** to the Father while they continued to live and serve Jesus throughout their lives upon this earth.*

Jesus' claim of being the only way to the Father can't have any connection to NAR's teaching on salvation for several reasons. First, and this is probably the most important point, *Jesus' statement does not require faith in Him.* He simply affirmed the fact that no one comes/goes to the Father except *through Him.* He did not

---

[1] John 13:33, 36-37.
[2] John 10:31.
[3] Lk. 4:28-30.
[4] Heb. 9:27.
[5] John 14:2-3.

say that no one comes/goes to the Father except *by believing in Him. A person does not have to believe in Jesus to have Jesus as the way to the Father.* He can have this way to the Father on an unconditional basis just because it has been provided for him by Jesus in His death upon the cross of Golgotha. God's love for all men made the cross sufficient for all men to have a relationship with God even without believing in Jesus.

NAR's teaching tells us quite plainly that a person is saved[1] by believing in Jesus.[2] But here in John 14:6 there is no requirement to believe in Jesus. Such a condition is typically *assumed* to be present, but a plain reading of the verse finds no such requirement at all. *If there is no need to believe in Jesus, then there can be no resulting salvation of the kind that NAR and most of modern day Christianity assume to be present in John 14:6.* On the other hand, Acts 16:30-31 is offering a salvation that requires faith in Jesus but it is not a rescue from hell or a deliverance into heaven as the broader context of the book of Acts explains.[3]

Furthermore, it is quite plain that a person is challenged to believe in Jesus in order to have eternal life,[4] the abundant life that Jesus was offering[5] as a foretaste of the kingdom experience[6] that He was going to set up[7] after a lengthy delay has occurred.[8] But

---

[1] Salvation is essentially defined in NAR as a gift that meets every need a person has in order for him to obtain heaven as his afterlife destiny.

[2] Acts 16:30-31. Most likely the salvation mentioned here in Acts 16:30-31 has nothing to do with the accepted soteriological concepts taught in NAR. This salvation is not about escaping hell or being delivered into heaven safely, concepts entirely absent not only from this context but from the whole Bible as well. This salvation is solely related to entering the coming kingdom of Messiah (being *rescued* from all danger and *being delivered into* the safety of the kingdom). Cf., Matt. 19:23-25; 24:13-14.

[3] Acts 15:1-11; 16:16-17.

[4] John 3:16; 6:47.

[5] John 10:10.

[6] Heb. 6:4-5.

[7] Matt. 3:2; 4:17, 23; 6:33; 7:21; Dan. 7:13-14, 27.

[8] Matt. 24:45—25:13.

never is a person challenged to believe in Jesus in order to get to heaven.

Note carefully that Jesus did not say that He *becomes the way* to the Father in heaven *if a person believes in Him*. He said that He *was the way* for all people whether or not they believe in Him. It should be plain to all that when Jesus says that *no one* can come unless he comes *through* Jesus, He is saying that *all* must come to the Father *through* Him. *No one* can come to God any other way; consequently, *all* must come the same way.

John 14:6 is structurally equivalent to Jesus' statement, "I am equal to the Father."[1] He is that (equal with the Father) whether a person believes it or not. In this same sense, Jesus is the exclusive way to the Father whether a person hears about it and believe in it or not.

The second reason that Jesus' claim of being the only way to the Father cannot have anything to do with the salvation that NAR sets forth seems to be one of the most overlooked facts in the NT. Let me bring it into focus by asking a question: "In what way was Jesus *the way for Himself* to go to the Father?" After all, Jesus is certainly talking about *His own going* to the Father and *the way that He will take* for that journey, right? He didn't for some reason ignore the relevance of the questions that Thomas asked Him, and Peter before that, and suddenly apply them to everyone else in the world, did He? If He did, why would He do that?

Thomas was clearly asking Jesus where *He* was going and the way *He* was going to take to get there. Only by taking this verse out of its context or by ignoring the primary focus of the context can one arrive at the view that it is talking about salvation in the

---

[1] John 10:30. Being one with the Father means being of the same nature as the Father (Phil. 2:5-8) and thus being equal with the Father (John 5:18). But there are still two distinct persons, the Father and the Son.

sense of the term found in NAR. *Jesus did not need to be saved in the traditional Christian sense in order to go to the Father. Neither does anyone else.* Neither salvation nor the overall message of the Bible is about going to heaven in the first place. As a result that idea shouldn't be read into this passage or any other.

Since the apostles could not go to the Father *in the way that Jesus was about to go*, the Father would have to come to them. And interestingly enough, He promises to do exactly that in John 14:21, 23 when Jesus said,

> "'He who has My commandments and keeps them, that one is the one who loves Me; and he who loves Me shall be *loved[1] by My Father, and I will love him*,[2] and will disclose (or manifest) Myself to him. . . . And Jesus answered and said to him, 'If anyone is loving Me, he will keep My word (while he is in the act of loving Me); and **My Father will love him, and to him[3] We will come, and make Our abode with him**." (my translation, emphases, and parentheses)

Even though Jesus was going away from the apostles, He was not going to leave them as orphans;[4] He was going to come to them spiritually along with His Father. While the apostles could not go at this time to their *abode* in the Father's house that Jesus was going to prepare for them, both the Father and Jesus promise to come to them and make their *abode* with them while they continued to minister for Them on earth.

This *spiritual coming to make an abode* with the apostles will most probably be accomplished through the ministry of the God's Spirit who will be given shortly after Jesus' ascension into heaven and who is brought into the conversation at this point in Jesus'

---

[1] The future tense here denotes certainty, not future time.
[2] Again, the point is certainty, not pointing to some unseen future time.
[3] "To him" is in the emphatic position drawing the focus of Jesus' promise: it is to this one, to the one who loves Jesus by keeping His word, and not to anyone else.
[4] John 14:18.

upper room discourse.[1] The great parable of the Vine and the Branches that comes up immediately in chapter fifteen focuses upon the result of this communion cultivated by the Father[2] and produced (by the Spirit[3]) from the life of Jesus.[4]

Rather than looking at a person's *initial union* to Jesus, John 14:6 deals with the issue of *communion*, an on-going fellowship with God for the one already walking with God. There is nothing here about evangelism in the traditional sense that NAR tries to defend.

John 14:6 does not establish the ubiquitous supposition that NAR tries to defend, namely, that *only through faith in Jesus* can a person obtain heaven. It simply does not broach that subject in any way. Not everyone, believers included, will get into the Father's house. Those who, like the apostles, have sought daily communion with the Father will get in. If Andrew, Peter, John, Philip, and Nathanael can be taken to represent all twelve of the apostles, then they sought this communion with the Father *before*[5] and *after*[6] they received eternal life from Jesus.

Being faithful and getting into the Father's house has nothing to do with being initially saved or with finding the right path to heaven as NAR supposes. *There is no path that gets a person to heaven!* Period.

John 14:6 is not related to Matt. 7:13-14 even though NAR assumes it is and, therefore, tries to tie them together. There are simply too many differences between the passages for them to be

---

[1] John 14:16-18, 25-26

[2] John 15:1.

[3] The reader should notice that all the fruit mentioned in chapter fourteen and fifteen of John's Gospel mirror the fruit of the Spirit listed by Paul in Gal. 5:22-23.

[4] John 15:4-5.

[5] Cf., John 17:2, 6, 9.

[6] Cf., John 17:6-8.

understood as parallel passages, the latter one supposedly amplifying the former one. And these differences are so major that an objective person should conclude that they give opposite messages rather than two variations of the same one.

While NAR deals with other passages that it hopes demonstrate that Jesus required everyone to believe in Him in order to go to heaven, that demonstration has not been successfully made at this point in its arguments. NAR has assumed what it should have proven, and it has expounded its theology rather than God's word.

# Chapter 8

# What Exactly Did Jesus Claim? Pt. 2

There are other classic verses that NAR uses to support its claim that no one gets to heaven apart from belief in Jesus. But unfortunately NAR's theology is guiding its interpretation and limiting it so that no interpretation can disagree with the theology that it brought to the text initially. Just as NAR did in its exposition of Matt. 7:13-14, it will do again and again in every passage it tries to expound. *It will teach its readers its theology rather than what the original authors meant to say.*

NAR has been trained to see the whole Bible through a certain theological perspective. I was trained the same way to see the same theology that NAR presents. It is an understatement to say that it has been difficult to pull away from my original training. But the more I studied the Biblical text independently, the more I saw the necessity for giving up ideas that kept me from seeing what was actually being said.

I hope you can do the same as we wade together into the rip tide of popular, theological opinion that forcefully pulls the unexpected swimmer further and further from the truth he seeks. May God help us to fight the current and find the truth that sets the heart free as it transforms the soul gradually.

## Belief and Forgiveness in John 8:24

NAR turns to one of the only two passages that relates belief in Jesus to forgiveness of sin, hoping to show by it that apart from faith in Jesus no one gets to heaven. His major *assumption,* or course, is that no one gets to heaven without the forgiveness that Jesus speaks of when He addresses the religious leaders. NAR says,

> "Even the Pharisees who worshiped the one true God, Yahweh, and attempted to follow His laws were not exempted from Jesus's condition for salvation."[1]

Before we get to the verse that NAR uses, which is John 8:24, the reader must have clearly understood that when NAR uses the term salvation, he is speaking of not only being forgiven of one's sins, and receiving Christ's own righteousness in the process (yes, this is identical to the traditional understanding of justification because NAR sees these terms as basic equivalents), but also of obtaining the guarantee of a heavenly destiny. So, to reject Jesus *supposedly* means to have no way to obtain forgiveness of sins, no other way to be righteous before God without the gift of Christ's righteousness, and no way to remove the penalty upon his sins that would assuredly send him to hell. This is the standard of acceptable belief according to NAR. Anything less than this is considered unbiblical and un-Christian.

But this belief fails to understand all the different ways that God has provided forgiveness for people throughout human history. None of the forgiveness given in OT times was ever *explicitly* related to a belief in Jesus (or to a belief in the coming Messiah). NAR also fails to bring into its discussion the fact that the religious leaders standing before Jesus could be (and probably were) without any other sin than that of rejecting Jesus at that moment. They could have obtained their forgiveness by offering the

---

[1] NAR, p. 92-93.

required sacrifice,[1] by repenting of their sins,[2] or by praying toward the temple as they sought personal forgiveness[3] (just to mention three of the various ways they could have obtained their forgiveness). There are several other ways as well, actually around ten or eleven to my accounting.

What about the righteousness that NAR thinks is needed to stand before God? Is belief in Jesus the only way to obtain the kind of righteousness that God would approve of? Or to say that in a little different way, is belief in Jesus the only way to obtain the righteousness that is *supposedly* needed to be acceptable to God?

If Zachariah and Elizabeth could be righteous by following the Law, and they were according to the *explicit* statement of the Scriptures,[4] so could the religious leaders standing before Jesus at this moment. NAR fails to appreciate the diligence involved in attempting to keep the Law *in order to follow God with your whole heart*.[5] The apostle Paul was crystal clear that he had obtained all the righteousness that the Law required, and he had obtained it *before* he ever trusted in Jesus.[6] It is possible, then, to be righteous and live righteously before God apart from believing in a coming Messiah or in Jesus, the Messiah who had come.

That only leaves the issue of heaven and hell. Forgiveness could have been obtained apart from faith in Jesus. Righteousness could have been obtained apart from faith in Jesus. Did you notice that John 8:24 says not one word about hell or about heaven? Furthermore, did you notice that the immediate context of John 8:24

---

[1] Lev. 4:20ff.
[2] Cf., Jonah 3:5—4:2.
[3] 1Kgs. 8:27-30.
[4] Lk. 1:6.
[5] Deut. 6:4-9; Ps. 19:7-14; Ps. 119:1-2; etc.
[6] Phil. 3:6-9.

never mentions salvation or the need to be saved in the sense that NAR is trying to require? Why should dying in one's sins, and we will see what that actually refers to in a moment, be connected to a person's eternal destiny in hell the way NAR does? It is so common to hear this motif in the sermons preached that no one ever stops to question it from the immediate context of the passage being expounded.

John 8:24, the thread that NAR uses to tie belief in Jesus to forgiveness of sins,[1] says,

> "I said therefore to you that you shall die in your sins; for unless you believe that I am *He*, you shall die in your sins."

To what sins was Jesus referring when He warned these religious leaders about dying in them? As I have indicated previously, these were *not all of their sins*, past, present, and future (as NAR's theology requires to be involved in the forgiveness transaction with God). These were only the sins of not believing that Jesus was *He*, namely, the Messiah sent from God. That is what Jesus was referring to when He said, "… unless you believe that I am *He*, you will die in your sins." Unless you believe that I am who? The Messiah sent from God.[2] The Prophet foretold by Moses who would be like Moses.[3] The Son of Man who would receive *a kingdom* from the Ancient of Days,[4] the God of Israel, to establish *that kingdom* upon the earth for Israel as God had promised.[5] That is the *He* Jesus meant.

The salient point here is that Jesus' words cannot fit into the widely held theology that NAR presents because the sins referred

---

[1] NAR could've used Acts 10:36-43. That will be dealt with under Peter's messages.

[2] John 7:16, 17, 28-29, 40-43; 8:2, 14-19.

[3] Deut. 18:18-20.

[4] Dan. 7:13-14. Cf., Lk. 1:32-33; 19:11-27.

[5] Isa. 2:1-4; 9:6-7; 11:1-16; Matt. 6:10.

to only involve those of accepting or rejecting Jesus as God's promised Messiah. Jesus is only warning the religious leaders about those sins and no others. The reason? The other sins would have been taken care of through several different means that God had ordained for His people. The religious leaders had no reason to be concerned about their other sins. But the sin of rejecting Jesus carried with it major consequences that could not be avoided.

Rejecting Jesus as the Messiah in the first century was an important sin. It was so important that it could lead to a tragic, but deserved physical death. Israel had a chance to be delivered from the hand of all their enemies through the Messiah Jesus. But if they rejected Him, their enemies would not be removed from ruling over them.[1] Instead, those enemies would even be allowed to destroy their nation completely.[2] This is, of course, what happened to Israel between A.D. 70-73. The forgiveness that Jesus was referring to was a limited one which, if it was not obtained, would lead to the nation's destruction.

It should be clear that the theology that NAR presents is actually *inherently contradictory* when it comes to forgiveness and belief in Jesus. One the one hand, it requires a forgiveness that includes *all the sins* that a person will *ever* commit. Yet, on the other hand, it requires a person to believe in Jesus in order to be forgiven (and go to heaven as a result). But if the person in the first century had been justified or saved (basically the same results spring from both of these phenomena according to NAR's theology) just before Jesus began His ministry, then he no longer has to believe in Jesus to be forgiven or to go to heaven. The reason? Because that "believer's" previous justification (or salvation)

---

[1] Lk. 1:68-71.
[2] Cf., Matt. 22:1-7.

would cover all of the future sins that he would commit. Consequently, he would be forgiven for rejecting Jesus (because it would be one of his future sins that would have been forgiven when he was first justified or saved) and, thereby, be qualified to go to heaven. In short, as far as all the people who were confronted with Jesus' ministry are concerned, *if justification or salvation included the forgiveness of all future sins, then there was no need to believe in Jesus to be forgiven or to go to heaven.* NAR's theology is self-defeating. With a continuously shrinking world, we need a better Christianity to present to our new neighbors.

## Matt. 25:31-46: The Sheep and the Goats

As NAR moves on to the issue of eternity, trying to prove that only those who believe in Jesus will end up in heaven, it makes this interesting statement:

> "... Jesus taught that there are two distinct possibilities for people's **eternal destination**. Christ drove a stake through the universalist theory that all people, regardless of their **faith**, will end up in heaven."[1] (emphasis mine)

NAR uses Matt. 25:46 as its proof text. This parable by Jesus of the sheep and the goats has given some of the best scholars problems since the Reformation. The reason that it has been so troublesome is that it simply doesn't fit into the traditional, orthodox paradigm very well (if at all).

There are at least six considerations that need to be presented fairly and objectively before any attempt to use this passage correctly is made. 1.) What is the meaning of *eternal*?[2] 2.) What does

---

[1] Jeffress, p. 99.

[2] It should be noted that there is no Hebrew or Greek term that is equivalent to our English terms *eternity* and *eternal*. NAR's comments reveal, not the truths of this passage, but those *supposed* facts formulated in the systematization of Christian theology.

*eternal life* refer to in this context? 3.) What is the condition that must be fulfilled for a person to have eternal life in this context? 4.) How are the circumstances, when these things take place, especially relevant to an understanding of eternal life? 5.) Since the kingdom is called eternal, how long of a time is designated for eternal in this passage? 6.) Finally, what was (or could have been) the *faith* (or the belief system) of the goats? The answers to these questions demonstrate the unlikelihood of NAR's arguments. *What the text actually says and what NAR has been trained to see in it can never be brought together* if it is interpreted fairly and objectively.

What are the answers to the six questions above? Very briefly they are as follows:

1.) The meaning of the term *eternal*, as always, is an indefinite length of time, but not a time without end.[1]

2.) Eternal life in this context, as in a few others, refers to the coming kingdom of Messiah (e.g., cf. Matt. 25:34 with 25:46; and see Mk. 10:30; Lk. 10:25-28). Don't try to force it to fit with John 3:16, for example, because it can't.

3.) The condition for obtaining the kingdom (eternal life) in this context is ministering to the Jewish people during their time of great turmoil. To use a familiar word then, we might say that the condition for obtaining eternal life (or for entering the kingdom of heaven) is *works*. Obtaining eternal life is based upon the works of service that a person does for the persecuted Jews. NAR is using this passage as proof that *faith* in Jesus is needed to end up in

---

[1] *Theological Workbook of the Old Testament*, editors: R. Laird Harris, Gleason Archer, Jr., Bruce K. Waltke. Moody Publishers, in two volumes; vol. 2, p. 673. After researching every use of the terms for *eternal* in both the OT and NT, I fully concur with them.

heaven. But the interpreter should notice that initial faith in Jesus is not even mentioned in this context!

4.) The opportunity for ministering to the Jewish people in their great distress during the time designated in the Bible as the Great Tribulation will arise when the whole world is consumed by wars. It will be a chaotic time with deadly consequences for any service given to the Jews.

5.) From Rev. 20:1-7 we know that the kingdom will be one thousand years in duration. Hence, *eternal* here refers to that length of time and no more.

6.) Both the sheep and the goats represent Gentile peoples. The content of their faith is not revealed here. We do not know from this context whether they had believed in Jesus or not. *It is their works that is the basis for their judgment* not their faith in (or rejection of) Jesus.

To summarize very briefly, it should be noticed that this parable portrays the final judgment of these *living* individuals. Furthermore, there is no mention of faith in Jesus as a condition for the salvation that NAR wants to find in the parable. Consequently, in the last judgment, there will be no need to have believed in Jesus. Notice also that there is no mention of heaven or of going to heaven in this passage. There is only mention of a kingdom of heaven which has come down to earth just as Jesus taught that it would.[1] This passage hardly supports the demand for faith in Jesus in order to go to heaven that NAR is seeking. All that NAR needs to be said in this passage must be added to it in order to establish its defense of Christian exclusivity.

---

[1] Matt. 6:10. See. Dan. 7:13-14, 27 also.

## Lk. 16:19-31: The Rich Man and Lazarus

As NAR continues trying to demonstrate that faith in Jesus is necessary to go to heaven, it uses Lk. 16:19-31, the parable (or actual lives) of the rich man and Lazarus. Just like NAR handled the last passage, it handles this one. Just like the ugly step-sisters tried to force Cinderella's shoe onto their feet, NAR tries to force this parable to fit its understanding of salvation (or justification). As a result, it skips over the details that demonstrate its misunderstanding and draws the conclusions that its theology requires it to draw.

Some of the questions that we ought to ask as we study this passage might be these:

1.) Like the last passage what is the basis for judgment in this passage[1] and how does that harmonize with NAR's teaching on salvation?

2.) How long did it take for the rich man to see the error of his past life?

3.) Is there reason to believe that he had spent his entire life not only living in the lap of luxury but also *justifying himself* and the lifestyle that he was living as he did so?[2]

4.) Would you call the rich man's response, the one he gave in hell, repentance?

5.) What is the content of the rich man's faith? Did that change after he got to hell?

6.) Would his change in beliefs and perspectives lessen his time in hell?

---

[1] For the context one should go back to verse fourteen at least, if not to verse one. The context is about being a lover of money, the handling of which illustrates the way a rich man could prepare for God's future judgment upon his delegated stewardships.
[2] Lk. 16:14-15.

What would this man have had to believe in order to be saved according to NAR's theology? The fact that Jesus doesn't even bring up what these two believed ought to be a red flag for the objective student of the Bible that the content of one's faith is not the basis for either the rich man's or Lazarus' judgment. What was the basis, according to Jesus' own words, for their respective destinies? The answer is obvious: *it is how each one handled the lot in life God had given him to lead!*

Second, what does the passage say about the length of time each one spends in the place where God had sent him? NAR concludes from this parable that hell is "an irrevocable destination (Luke 16:26)."[1] Does the text *actually* say that or is that NAR's *theological accounting* of the passage? NAR declares its theological understanding of the teaching of the parable with these words:

> "Once a person dies and finds him – or herself in this place of *eternal punishment*, Jesus said, *all opportunity for faith and repentance are over*."[2] (emphases mine)

> "Those who teach that hell … is only a temporary location, where occupants will have an opportunity to trust in Christ and experience deliverance from God's judgment, must completely dismiss Jesus's teaching that *hell is a forever destination*."[3]

Is this what the passage *explicitly* says or has NAR added a layer of errant interpretation on top of the text that would surely mislead others? Nothing in the context forbids the idea that once the rich man's punishment had accomplished its remedial purpose, he can then move out of hell, not temporarily for relief, but permanently since his restoration (reconciliation) and refinement (transformation) have been completed. What good news!

---

[1] NAR, p. 100.
[2] Ibid.
[3] Ibid, p. 101.

Remember the rich man's sin was one of omission, not using his wealth to help Lazarus (and those like him). He failed to righteously perform the stewardship that God had given him to oversee. This vignette from Jesus' teaching might not be a parable at all. It might be Jesus' way of illustrating the truth that He would give four to nine months later[1] about how difficult it is for a rich man to enter the kingdom of heaven,[2] using an actual example from life. If a person today isn't a good steward[3] of the wealth God enabled him to obtain,[4] then he will, apparently, follow this rich man to hell regardless of whether he has believed in Jesus.

It should also be noted that the length of time it took the rich man to repent in hell was extremely short. If God's chastisements are remedial, producing a remedy for sins and sinfulness,[5] then how long do you suspect the rich man stayed in hell?[6] His repentance is evident by the way Jesus tells the story.

If you had to write the end of Jesus' parable, how would you end it? Would you conclude with NAR that all opportunity for repentance and faith are over once a person arrives in hell? Would you conclude that the rich man, regardless of his repentance, had to stay in hell for the rest of his existence? How would you portray God as just in this matter? As merciful? Loving?

Several facts lead us to a different interpretation of Jesus' parable than the one traditionally accepted. First, since the term

---

[1] *Jesus Christ The Greatest Life*, a unique blending of the four gospels. Complied and translated by Johnston M. Cheney and Stanley Ellisen; Paradise Publishing Company, 1999, p. 138.

[2] Mk. 10:23-25.

[3] Lk. 12:16-21.

[4] Deut. 8:11-20.

[5] Cf., Dan. 9:24-25; Heb. 12:4-13.

[6] Should hell be seen as an experience of the love of God (rather than the wrath of God which is never connected to hell in the Bible) for the purpose of producing righteousness (Heb. 12:4-13)?

*eternal* in Greek and Hebrew is not synonymous to that term in English, no one should understand them with an English meaning. Hell is not an endless experience of punishment. Since that is true, what happens to the rich man once he has repaid his debt to God,[1] becoming in the process what God intended him to be?[2]

Second, there is repentance and refinement achieved today[3] as well as in the future[4] through the trials that God brings upon this earth. Sometimes Jesus uses what happens in this life as a template for what is going to happen in the life after death.[5] It should be an expectation that there will be this kind of refinement in the afterlife, a refinement that produces repentance[6] and conformity to the image of Jesus Christ and to the will of the Father.[7] Jesus' payment *for all* of man's sins obviously doesn't ameliorate a person's judgment in the afterlife.

Third, after the *recompense* has been paid for the sins committed,[8] God would be unjust to keep a person any longer in hell since there is no such thing as an *eternal* penalty (that would confuse the English with the Greek and Hebrew once again) for any personal sin that an individual might commit. These principles seem to be exactly what Jesus was trying to communicate to the apostles when he answered Peter's question about forgiving another person.[9] The whole concept of *an eternal penalty*[10] is a

---

[1] Cf., Matt. 18:34-35.
[2] Cf., Ps. 119:67, 71, 75; Heb. 12:7-13; 1Pet. 1:6-7; Js. 1:2-4.
[3] Js. 1:2-4.
[4] Dan. 9:24-25; Matt. 11:25; Lk. 12:41-48.
[5] Matt. 18:21-35.
[6] Lk. 16:24, 27-31.
[7] Js. 1:4; 1Pet. 1:6-7.
[8] 2Cor. 5:10.
[9] Matt. 18:34-35.
[10] The reference to an "eternal punishment" in Matt. 25:46 is naturally taken to coincide with the time frame of the kingdom, which is mentioned in v. 34 and which is being missed. Thus, eternal is not an indeterminate period. Rather, it seems to denote a point in

misunderstanding of the teaching of the Bible on several levels.

Fourth, there are passages that say that everyone who has ever lived will fall on his knees and worship God.[1] *This is universal worship of the one true God.* While such worship is the entreaty of the OT,[2] it is the predicted reality of the NT.[3] Even the wicked dead will come to this point eventually.

Repentance and faith in God which lead to the worship of God would make God appear to be conscientiously unjust if He were to keep those in hell who have come to that place in their lives. Since there is no passage that actually says that all who go to hell are there for the rest of their existence, it would be more consistent to see the experience of hell as being remedial just like most of the trials that God brings (or allows) into people's lives while they live on earth.[4] Since all men are His sons, He is working to bring all the prodigals back into fellowship with Him.

Of course, it is possible that some might be in hell for a much longer time than others (which time frame is not disclosed to us in the Scriptures). But the decision by God upon the use of hell in a person's life will not be based upon the simple formula that we have heard so often, namely, belief in Jesus keeps one from hell; rejection of Jesus sends one to hell. It's just not like that.

If faith in Jesus is the only way for a person to obtain heaven as his eternal destiny, as NAR says that it is as it presents the mainline, evangelical belief within Christendom today, then the vast majority of people, that God created and placed upon this earth, were placed here just to wind up in hell afterwards. NAR

---

time beyond which someone or something will not go. Cf., Rev. 20:13, 15 which allow for this possibility suggested here.

[1] Phil. 2:8-11; Rev. 5:13-14.

[2] E.g., Ps. 66:1; Ps. 67:1-3.

[3] E.g., Phil. 2:9-11; Rev. 5:13.

[4] Js. 1:2-4; 1Tim. 1:18-20; Ps. 119:67, 71, 75.

says that while that may be troubling to some, if it is what Jesus taught, then that is the way it is.[1] I agree. If Jesus had taught that scenario, then that would be the way it will be. But He didn't teach that scenario. *Man has come up with that horrific scenario; it did not come from God.*

Only by making words say what they don't really mean can a person come up with this demeaning characterization of God. You can easily determine what all the important terms mean by using an English concordance and looking up every usage of each term. Keep a journal about what each term means in each context. This is not beyond your ability to do. Gather together a group of like-minded people who are willing to give up everything they have been taught in order to finally understand the message of the Bible correctly. You will surprise yourself. But you will end up with different ideas from those you have been taught to this point. Seek truth because only truth will set you free.

We've looked at the classic passages that NAR uses to prove that Jesus required every person to believe in Him in order to be forgiven, in order to be righteous before God, and in order to go to heaven when he died. But what we found is that Jesus never made such demands on anyone. Where does that leave us? We must conclude that *God has a very different way to be acceptable to Him, a way that is available to all men alike.* Now the task must be to discover that pathway, a road that doesn't lead to heaven, but rather to the heart of God.[2]

---

[1] NAR, pp. 101-102.

[2] See my book, *A Shrinking World Requires a Better Christianity* and the chapter on the "Universal Will of God." It will be an eye-opener.

# Chapter 9

# The Teachings of the Apostle Peter
on the exclusivity of Christianity, Pt. 1

We have just reviewed the classic verses spoken by Jesus that NAR uses to support the idea that having faith in Jesus is the only way a person can get to heaven. We have found that when these verses are studied without the constraints of NAR's theological grid, they do not support the ideas attributed to them; they do not teach that faith in Jesus is the only way a person can get to heaven. If this idea didn't come directly from the mouth of Jesus, then from whom did it come?

We must now turn to Peter's classic comments that NAR has taken to support the teaching that belief in Jesus is the only guarantee for a heavenly destiny. Will we find that they clearly support that doctrine? If Jesus never communicated that idea, it will be unusual to find it in Peter's or in Paul's messages. But let us be certain that this doctrine of exclusivity is either taught by those preeminent apostles or is, in fact, an errant belief that we ourselves have manufactured.

## Peter's Sermon at Pentecost

NAR begins with a discussion of Acts 2:37 and Peter's sermon on the first Pentecost after Jesus' ascension. Peter had just explained how the miraculous languages that were being spoken and Jesus' resurrection prove His Messiahship. At the end of his sermon, the multitude realized that they had crucified the

121

Messiah that God had sent to them. The whole multitude, it seems, was under great conviction. They said to Peter, and to the apostles who stood with him,

"Brethren, what shall we *do*?" (Acts 2:37, emphasis mine)

It is easy to see their dilemma. Since they had crucified the Messiah who was supposed to set up their promised kingdom, what could they now do to resurrect God's plan for Israel (pun intended)? But NAR takes this episode in an entirely different direction. It tries to make Peter's sermon fit the salvation from hell and the guarantee of heaven motif. As a result, NAR asks,

"*Do*? Why would members of the 'house of Israel' need to do anything? After all, they were already part of God's chosen nation. The males would have been circumcised. They regularly offered sacrifices as the Old Testament prescribed. *Was Peter implying that their sincerely held Jewish beliefs were not enough? Apparently so*…. The heart of the message was that everyone – Jews included – must *trust in Jesus Christ for the forgiveness of sins*."[1] (emphases mine)

Is NAR correct? Was this what Peter was saying? And, if we get ahead of ourselves just a little, was this what Paul later said in Acts 24:14-16 and in Phil. 3:6? Take a look:

"But this I admit to you, that according to the Way which they call a sect I do serve the God of our fathers, *believing everything that is in accordance with the Law, and that was written in the Prophets*; having a hope in God which these men cherish themselves, that *there shall certainly be a resurrection* of both the righteous and the wicked. *In view of this, I also do my best to maintain always a blameless conscience both before God and before men.*" (Acts 24:14-16, emphases mine)

And,

"… as to zeal, a persecutor of the church; *as to the righteousness which is in the Law, found blameless.*"

---

[1] NAR, p. 117.

Was there some deficiency in what the Jews believed before Jesus came on the scene as NAR suggests? What exactly would that have been? Paul's personal testimonies certainly don't seem to be saying that there was any deficiency in the OT system. Since it was given by God for the purpose of guiding the Jewish people in a detailed walk with Him, why would anyone ever suspect that the OT was in any way inadequate in accomplishing the purpose God designed it to accomplish? Isn't NAR basically suggesting that God made a mistake in giving the OT Law in the first place?

The typical Jew believed in the God of the OT, the God of Israel who had revealed Himself by different names at different times in the history of the nation.

He believed that God had given revelation to Moses, and he believed in the history of Israel recorded in the OT.

He believed, furthermore, that his God was sending a Messiah, an anointed Savior, to deliver the nation from the hand of all who hate them. This same Messiah would establish a kingdom for them that would *never end*, one that would last *as long as life on this earth endured*.

All of these things can be easily discovered by just a cursory reading of the Gospels. The typical Jew was even expecting the Messiah to come at this point in time. But he didn't anticipate any changes in his personal life (repentance and the need to turn away from sin) or in his religious life (the Law would be set aside as the OT had foretold). In short, the typical Jew's belief system was exactly what it should have been, namely, *what God told them it should be*.

So, Peter was not implying that their belief system was in any way inadequate or insufficient as NAR suggests. If Jesus had not arrived on the scene, the typical Jew would have gone to heaven, even though that is not the message of the Bible or the ultimate desire of the people in the OT, and would have been judged relative to the stewardships that God had given him to oversee. The result of that judgment would have determined his experiences from that point forward. His hope would have been that he would be counted worthy to participate in the kingdom program that the Messiah would eventually set up on earth. The same scenario is true of every Christian today.

Did John the Baptist, Jesus, the apostles, or the NT prophets ever condemn or depreciate *the belief system* (the personal faith of the typical Jew) during this time? Not once. Rather, their message had to do with bringing the works of the individual up to the standard of righteous living. *The Jewish people at the time of Jesus' ministry, like Christians today, often did not consistently live up to what they believed.* This is the reason that the most prominent message to the Jews throughout the Gospels is "Repent for the Kingdom of Heaven is at hand."[1] The Jewish people needed to rethink how they were living because they were not living up to the standard that had been given to them in their OT Scriptures. Only righteous people will be able to enter the kingdom when it is finally set up. This righteousness cannot be given; it must be sought[2] and achieved by obedience performed in dependence upon God.[3]

After Jesus' crucifixion, resurrection, and ascension, the content of the message that the apostles preached did not change from the message that Jesus had preached throughout His entire earthly ministry (except, or course, the resurrection was added to it[4]). The message was still "Repent for the Kingdom can still be

---

[1] E.g., Matt. 3:2; 4:17: 11:20-24.
[2] Matt. 6:33.
[3] Rom. 1:5; Js. 2:22, 24. Cf., also, Matt. 8:5-13; Lk. 8:11-16.
[4] Mk. 16:1-20; Acts 17:30-34; etc.

established when King Jesus returns to earth." That hope can be found in Acts 3:18-26 just as clearly as it can be found in Jesus' sermons during His earthly ministry.

Generally speaking, repentance related to what they were *doing, not* to what they were *believing* when Jesus first came upon the scene. The apostle Paul *explicitly* confirms this perspective in the passage quoted above, Acts 24:14-16. In addition, Paul also said in Phil. 3:6 that *following in faith what he had believed as a typical Jew of his day made him righteous before God.* Needless to say, there is no improvement needed upon that standard of living. Most Christians today wish they could make such a statement about themselves.

Peter's Pentecostal sermon in Acts 2:37-40 is identical to John the Baptist's message when he came upon the scene. They both required their audiences to repent and to be baptized for the forgiveness of their sins. It would have been natural to expect Peter to have said, "Believe on the Lord Jesus Christ and be forgiven of your sins," if faith in Jesus was ever a means of obtaining forgiveness. But he doesn't say that, and everyone ought to ask, "Why didn't Peter simply tell his audience that faith in Jesus is all anyone needed to obtain forgiveness of all sins?" Peter preached the gospel of the kingdom message, not the gospel of grace message which is set forth as the only faithful message of the Bible. I have not found that such a view can pass the test of independent scrutiny.

In the end Peter's Pentecostal sermon doesn't provide any support for NAR's belief that faith in Jesus is the only way to be forgiven and, therefore, the only way to get to heaven. Peter certainly did not promote such an idea. He does, however add the promise of the Holy Spirit to those who would repent concerning their former reject of Jesus and be baptized. By these two responses each person could receive forgiveness for rejecting Jesus as Messiah and the Holy Spirit who would enable them to live a righteous life moving forward. But Peter never once preached NAR's message for the simple reason that forgiveness is not obtained by believing in Jesus.

## Peter's Explanation of Acts 4:12

NAR uses Acts 2:37 in an attempt to demonstrate the inadequacies of Israel's beliefs as far as going to heaven is concerned. It *assumes* the Jews fell short of pleasing God wholly because they had rejected Jesus. But neither the Jews nor Jesus was in the least concerned about going to heaven. Their concern centered almost entirely upon doing God's will upon this earth[1] so that entrance into the prophesied kingdom could be gained.[2] Obtaining entrance into the coming kingdom is not a grace issue. Rather, it is dependent upon works,[3] developing the proper dispositions,[4] and faithfulness to the opportunities that have been given to a person for service.[5]

NAR *assumes* that obtaining an all-encompassing, once-for-all forgiveness for every sin a person would ever commit is a key and basic requirement for going to heaven, for salvation.

It further *assumes* that this forgiveness is *only available* to those who believe in Jesus.

Consequently, after showing the need for forgiveness in Acts 2:38, NAR moves to the classic passage of Acts 4:12 in an attempt

---

[1] Relate Matt. 6:10 to Matt. 7:21-27. Cf., also, Matt. 12:50; 21:28-32; Lk. 10:25-27.

[2] Matt. 5:20; 7:21; 18:3.

[3] Rev. 22:12; Mk. 10:17-30; Col. 3:23-25; 2Cor. 5:10.

[4] Matt. 5:3-12; 18:3.

[5] Matt. 20:1-16, esp. v. 7.

to tie three threads together: the need of forgiveness to go to heaven, the need of believing in Jesus to be forgiven, and the concept of salvation. By tying these three threads together, NAR tries to establish Peter's belief in the exclusivity of faith in Jesus as the only way to heaven. NAR's logic goes like this:

Unless one is forgiven, he cannot go to heaven.

Unless one believes in Jesus, there is no forgiveness of sins and, consequently, no salvation (which is generally limited to the idea of going to heaven).

NAR's hope is that Acts 2:38 and Acts 4:12 lay an unshakable foundation for tying these three convictions together.

While taking the context back to chapter three as it ought to do, NAR seems to be totally unaware of, or confused about, the point that Peter was making. In Peter's sermon he asked the crowd to do two things: repent and return. It seems most likely that Peter was asking these Jews in Jerusalem to reconsider the possibility that Jesus was their Messiah just as he had done in his earlier sermon at Pentecost. And after that thorough reconsideration gains them a proper perspective, he invited them to return to the God of Israel as the Shepherd of their souls[1] and to trust in Jesus as the promised Messiah who will become the good Shepherd[2] in His ministry to Israel. Like Father, like Son![3]

This seems to be the message that Paul preached during all of his missionary journeys[4] and probably should be understood as Peter's basic message as well. *Repentance* toward God and *faith* in (God who had given covenants and promises concerning the Messiah He would send and in) Jesus the Messiah who had come

---

[1] Gen. 48:15-16. Cf., 1Pet. 2:20-25.
[2] John 10:11-18.
[3] Cf., Matt. 9:35-36; Heb. 1:1-3.
[4] Acts 20:21.

to do the will of His heavenly Father. We must remember that all of the apostles agreed on the message when they met together with Paul in Jerusalem.[1] And Luke clearly delineates that message as one of repentance and forgiveness of sins offered in the name of Jesus who was the Christ.[2]

Peter connected the forgiveness of sins that the multitude needed directly to their rejection of Jesus as God's Messiah. The crowd's other sins had been touched upon in both Jesus' and John the baptizer's earthly ministry as they both preached repentance and baptism as a means to obtain forgiveness.[3] So, the forgiveness that the crowd needed was *not a comprehensive forgiveness of all of their sins over their whole lives*. Even less likely would anyone in the crowd be expecting the forgiveness to reach into the future for sins they had yet to commit.[4] Peter is certainly not *explicitly* offering such a total and all-encompassing forgiveness. And it is only that all-encompassing kind of forgiveness that NAR's theology needs in order to make its concept of salvation work. Either all sins must be forgiven at the same time, or there can be no salvation/justification at all.

When NAR attempts to explain Acts 4:12, it focuses upon verse ten in order to connect the man's healing with *the sermon* that Peter had just given the day before. In both cases, in his sermon the day before and now in his defense before the Sanhedrin, Peter referred to the death and resurrection of Jesus. NAR sees these references as a sign that Peter was giving *the traditional Christian understanding of the gospel* in both cases.

---

[1] Gal. 2:6-10.

[2] Lk. 24:47. Whether the text is repentance *and* forgiveness or repentance *for* forgiveness there is no distinction to be made based upon Luke's perspective on these things.

[3] Cf., Mk. 1:3-4; Matt. 3:2; 4:17; John 3:22-23; 4:1-2; Mk. 16:15-16.

[4] All of Israel's provisions for sins only dealt with those which were already committed. None dealt with the future sins or the penalties upon them that they might commit.

For NAR, 1Cor. 15:3-5 was going through Peter's mind, and his message was one of being saved from hell and of being given heaven as a free gift through the forgiveness that is obtained by faith in Christ Jesus. But the major problem with this interpretation is that *forgiveness of all past, present, and future sins was never offered for faith in Jesus Christ.* Jesus Himself never taught that forgiveness could be obtained by believing in Him. Not even 1Cor. 15:3-5 teaches this idea. So, from where does this concept of forgiveness arise?

When NAR expounds upon Acts 4:12, it throws its expositional net over chapters three and four, trapping such items as forgiveness, the death and resurrection of Jesus, the terms saved and salvation, and the need to believe in Jesus. Regardless of whether the terms are syntactically related or not, it suggests that the traditional doctrine of salvation from hell must be the issue being preached.

Without denying that Peter challenged the crowd in the temple to repent and return to God (the term *conversion* is hardly appropriate here!), the central focus of chapter three and the first part of chapter four of Acts is clearly upon the healing of the lame man. It is that healing that amazed the crowds and stirred their interest. It was also the issue of this man's healing about which Peter and John had to give an account before the Sanhedrin. It is transparently obvious that Peter was not defending the sermon that he had preached the day before. Rather, he was explaining the healing that had taken place. It was the healing that aroused interest in Peter and John.

If the person, studying this passage, connects Acts 3:6, 12, 16 with Acts 4:8-10, he would see the overall context that is needed to properly interpret Acts 4:12. The correlation is quite obvious.

| | |
|---|---|
| v. 6 In *the name* of Jesus Christ | |
| v.12 Not by our own *power* or authority | v. 7 By what *power* or *name* |
| v.16 *His name* has **strengthened** this man | v.9 By what means he has been *made well* (saved!) |
| v.16 Through faith in *His name* his **soundness** was given | v.10 By *the name* of Jesus Christ |

Then Peter concluded his explanation to the Sanhedrin by saying,

> "And there is **salvation** (that is, **healing**) in no one else; for there is **no other name** under heaven that has been given among men by which we must be **saved** (that is, **healed**)." (Acts 4:12, emphases and parentheses mine)

It should be manifestly clear that the salvation that Peter is talking about is the physical healing that had occurred in the life of this lame man. In the immediate context, verse nine of chapter four of Acts, the term *saved* is used and can only be properly understood as the lame man's physical healing. Consequently, Acts 4:12 has nothing at all to do with the traditional understanding of *spiritual* salvation. No one is being saved from hell; no one is being given the free gift of a heavenly destiny. This verse is solely about the healing that had taken place.

NAR believes that Peter's statement in Acts 4:12

> "forever closed the door on the mistaken concept that other religions *worship the same Jesus* but call Him by a different name?"[1]

While that name in Acts 4:12 is certainly Jesus (of Nazareth), it is given for healing the sick, not for getting the healthy to heaven.[2]

---

[1] NAR, p. 119.

[2] While it is not our purpose to pursue every exclusivistic thought that NAR sets forth, it should be noted that in Gen. 20:1-11 Abraham and Abimelech knew the one true God by different names (Elohim and Adonai, respectively). Also in Ps. 65:2, the psalmist clearly says that all men *pray* to the same God and 65:5 adds that they *trust* in God when they pray to Him.

Furthermore, it is not being debated by this writer that all religions worship the same *Jesus*. The debate is whether they could be worshipping the same God who is Father over all. Not even the Jews, who were acceptable before God in the OT, worshipped Jesus. But they did worship the one, true God as did Abimelech and his entire nation.[1]

Consequently, the debate is whether all men might worship *God the Father* by a different name.[2] *It is a fact of the OT that God did reveal Himself to different peoples by different names.* The reason this idea causes such spiritual heartburn today is that it takes away from Christianity the exclusive way to heaven that it has enjoyed having for over five hundred years. The passages are clear; it is our theology that is keeping us from understanding them correctly.

At this point NAR has marshalled no support from Peter to prove that only by believing in Jesus can a person be forgiven of his sins and go to heaven when he dies. But Peter's best lesson is yet to come. What Peter teaches the world in Acts 10-11 ought to settle the whole debate. If Acts ten had been properly understood, it is likely that NAR might never have been written.

---

[1] Gen. 20:1-11.

[2] Micah 4:5 affirms that God can be known and worshipped by other names. This will continue when Jesus has taken control and begin to reign over the whole earth. The context of Micah 4:5 is the Messianic Kingdom promised to the Jews as Is. 2:1-4, Micah's parallel passage, clearly confirms. In this kingdom all men walk righteously before God. They walk righteously, but they continue to call upon God by the name that they had known Him throughout their earthly lives.

132

# Chapter 10

# The Teachings of the Apostle Peter
# on the exclusivity of Christianity, Pt. 2

Peter's interaction with Cornelius in Acts ten is so important that it deserves its own chapter. If the reader is interested in the *universal will of God* for all people regardless of where they live or what religion they may be a part of, I hope he will read my book, *A Shrinking World Requires a Better Christianity*. In that book I devote an entire chapter to the demonstration from both Testaments that God has a universal will. If a person is obedient to that will, he will be pleasing to God throughout his life on earth and will be confident to stand before God's Judgment Seat for his final judgment. Acts 10-11 is a big piece of that evidence for a universal will of God. So it comes as no surprise that it simply cannot be harmonized with NAR's faithful presentation of the evangelical doctrine of salvation. The shoe of traditional, Christian soteriology, regardless of whether it is Calvinistic or Arminian, Catholic or Protestant, or some variation of them, just doesn't fit.

## Peter's New Understanding of the Gentiles

When NAR finally gets to the story of Cornelius in Acts 10-11, it opens its exposition of this episode in Peter's life by saying,

> "One of the clearest arguments for the necessity of *personal faith* in Christ for *salvation* is found in Peter's role in the *conversion* of the Roman centurion named Cornelius."[1]

---

[1] NAR, p. 119.

We must not lose sight of the fact that for NAR, salvation is a term that describes several necessary beliefs such as:

being forgiven of all one sins, past, present, and future
being given Christ's righteousness
being permanently declared to be forever right with God
being promised a place in heaven because of all of the above

And the only way to obtain these things is to believe in Jesus for them. NAR is clear in claiming that none of these things can come any other way. It is this way, by believing in Jesus, or hell.

The reader must not be confused at this point. I would agree with NAR that Jesus came to save His people from their sins and that this salvation takes place as a person believes in Him.[1] But I don't believe that salvation or justification involve any of the elements listed above that NAR and the theology that it represents include in these concepts.

No evangelical Christian should have a problem with NAR's understanding of salvation *if* the Bible *clearly and explicitly* sets it forth as *"the faith once for all delivered to the saints."*[2] But what if these things are the creation of man rather than the declarations of God?

If you haven't read Acts 10:1—11:18 recently, then that is the first thing you must do. Compare what NAR says about Cornelius and his faith with what Luke, under the inspiration of the Holy Spirit, says.

Are Cornelius' *sins* even an issue in this story?
Is he identified as righteous *before* or *after* believing in Jesus?
Was he *acceptable* to (welcomed by) God *before* or *after* he believed in Jesus?
Is a *heavenly destiny* mentioned?

---

[1] Matt. 1:21; John 10:27-28; 20:31.
[2] Jude 3.

Is *heaven* the focus of attention in any way?

Lastly, where is the concept of *conversion* introduced in this context?

NAR does not explain the text of Acts 10-11 to its readers; it expounds upon its theology, giving its readers the impression that the text is teaching its theological perspective when it doesn't.

While focusing upon Acts 10:1-2, NAR *presumes* to answer for the average person on the street the question about Cornelius' prospect of going to heaven when he died. Remember: there is no mention of heaven or hell in this context. Nor is there any desire on the part of anyone mentioned in this episode of going there. NAR is reading these ideas into the text because its concept of salvation requires them. As a result, NAR says,

> "If you asked the average person on the street if someone who believed in God, prayed regularly, and gave money to the poor would be *welcomed into heaven* when he died, the overwhelming majority of people would answer, 'Without a doubt!'"[1] (emphasis mine)

I used to completely disregard those who gave answers similar to what NAR describes here. I ignored such opinions as unchristian and unbiblical responses. Now I continue to believe that such a response is fully unchristian, but it is not necessarily unbiblical. I should have been listening to all those people, coming from different economic, social, and religious backgrounds. Furthermore, I should have been wondering about my own convictions as much as theirs. When I finally started to do that, I was astounded from the very beginning about how little Biblical support I had for my convictions. When we remain among likeminded people, our own convictions are rarely ever challenged.

Even when Luke gives such a glowing description of Cornelis' character, faith, and devotion, NAR concludes that he just

---

[1] NAR, p. 119.

didn't have enough to "secure his eternal salvation."[1] But what was God's opinion about Cornelius? What was Peter's? *God had to reveal His opinion to Peter in the vision of the sheet coming down out of heaven before Peter got to Cornelius' house in order to keep him from having the same opinion that NAR expresses.* I guess that means that most Christians could use a sheet-out-of-heaven-filled-with-unclean-animals vision today!

While Peter didn't understand the vision at first, by the time he heard all the testimony about Cornelius, and, most importantly, *before* he ever preached Jesus to him, he fully understood it. *The miraculous vision was to teach him about God's inclusivity of all mankind.* All men are acceptable individuals, welcomed to God, if they simply do two things: *fear God and do what is right!*

Isn't that exactly what Peter says in Acts 10:34-35? Doesn't his declaration recognize Cornelius' relation to the one true God?[2] The only reason that NAR doesn't deal with Acts 10:34-35 anywhere in its book is that these verses contradict NAR's message and, therefore, the basic premise of the book. *It is a simple fact that NAR simply cannot harmonize these two verses with its own teachings.*

NAR, as others have done before it, tries to make its theology fit the Cornelius episode by focusing upon Acts 10:36-43, especially verses forty-two and forty-three. But that focus does not provide the evidence needed to convinced the reader who is looking carefully at what Peter was saying. Acts 10:36-43 are not speaking about a message that was applicable to Cornelius and his household. They describe what was taking place in Jerusalem and specifically to the Jewish people who had first rejected Jesus, but who afterward received Him as their Messiah. Cornelius had

---

[1] NAR, p. 120.
[2] Cf., Acts 10:1-4, 22 with Acts 10:34-35.

never even heard of Jesus up to this point in his life. He, therefore, could not have rejected Jesus and be in need of forgiveness for that sin.

God had commissioned the apostles and those in the upper room to preach to those in Jerusalem first, and then, as the movement progressed outward from there, to go to the uttermost end of the world.[1] So Peter was speaking about the message that had been proclaimed to Israel about the One whom they had crucified. The person they had crucified had been appointed by God as the Judge of the living and the dead. Consequently, all the New Testament prophets bore witness concerning Jesus that *all who had rejected Him, if they repented and accepted Him, would have the sins involved in their initial rejection of Jesus forgiven them.* God had already provided forgiveness for their other sins in various ways.[2]

Because NAR misunderstands the place of forgiveness in God's plan and wrongly equates salvation with acceptance by God, it is hopelessly at odds with the text of Acts 10-11. Having become attached to the Jewish faith and being witnessed to as righteous and God fearing, Cornelius would have experienced forgiveness in the same ways that God had ordained for the Jewish people to obtain it, namely, through the sacrificial system and possibly also through prayer to Israel's God (as well as through repentance among several other options). Consequently, *Cornelius would have had no need for forgiveness at this point* as far as we know from the inspired text of Scripture which is supposed to be our guide for understanding this episode in the life of the early church. Since the passage never broaches forgiveness, nor

---

[1] Acts 1:8.
[2] See my book *The Grand Spiritual Assumption* which discusses several ways during this time that God had ordained for forgiveness to be obtained. Never was belief in Jesus, however, one of them.

especially Cornelius' need of one, it is appropriate not to require what the text doesn't require.

Cornelius was *already acceptable* before God *before* he trusted in Jesus. That is the plain conclusion one reaches when he connects Acts 10:1-4, 22 with Acts 10:34-35. Hence, the conclusion that Peter had just drawn and the one that Luke is requiring his readers to accept as well is the fact that *all men in every nation who fear God (as Cornelius did) and who do what is right (as Cornelius must have been doing to be described as righteous) are acceptable to God even though they might never have heard of Jesus, believed in Him, or been saved by Him.*[1] This is God's opinion, and it directly contradicts NAR's opinion and every other traditional, accepted theology that agrees with NAR.

Because of its commitment to a certain theological perspective, NAR is unable to draw the conclusion that Peter is actually setting before his audience. As a result, it asks,

"... is Cornelius in *a right relationship with God* even though he has *never trusted in Jesus Christ?*" (emphases mine)

Peter, bolstered by his recent, miraculous vision, would have emphatically answered that question with a resounding "Yes!" He even did that as Acts 10:34-35 explicitly states. But NAR is kept from seeing the obvious truth because it has been blinded by the theology that it has learned. Its theology is keeping it from understanding the message that the text is actually clearly teaching. I had the same problem about fifteen years ago. Praise God for the eye salve that Jesus gives to those who want to follow Him with their whole hearts. [2] As I had to learn, following orthodox

---

[1] Biblically speaking, this salvation would have been future like the one in Acts 16:30-31. They both refer to a deliverance (or salvation) into the Messianic kingdom when it is set up in the future upon Jesus' return to earth.
[2] Rev. 3:17-18.

theology is not the same thing as following the Bible.

The really sad thing about all of this is that NAR's message is hopelessly confused at this point. It is unable to see any purpose at all for Peter to have made the trip to share Jesus with Cornelius if Cornelius was already in a right relationship with God. NAR, unfortunately, reflects the futility of the Christian faith possessed by all too many Christians when it says:

> "... Peter made a wasted trip to Caesarea to preach to Cornelius, along with his family and friends."[1]

NAR even suggests that Peter's sermon would have been offensive to Cornelius because it assumes that Cornelius' religious beliefs were inferior to Peter's when they actually weren't.[2] But such thinking is *non-sequitur* at best. Because of wrongly equating being *acceptable* (or in a right relationship with God) with being *saved*, NAR confuses two very different issues and changes the message of the Bible in the process. *The message of the Bible does not reveal the right path to heaven; it describes the right path to walk to have fellowship with the God of heaven.*

NAR is not alone in thinking that salvation and evangelism have the goal of getting a person to heaven. So, if that is not the real purpose of sharing one's faith in Jesus, what good is it to be involved in missions? I was just at a national Christian conference at which I met a pastor who asked the very same question that NAR is asking here, namely, "If sharing Jesus with others is not about offering them a way to heaven, then why make the effort to share your faith at all. Aren't you really wasting your time and your money?"

I have answered these questions in detail in my recent book,

---

[1] NAR, p. 121.
[2] Ibid.

*A Shrinking World Requires a Better Christianity.* So, a brief answer to these questions will have to be sufficient for now. Jesus never offered heaven as a free gift. In fact, He never offered a destiny to heaven or a place in heaven or an eternity with God (however one may like to phrase it). What He offered was an extraordinary life that could be lived right now. That life would be the answer to all the trials and ills that befall mankind throughout his entire life. And that life would be a taste of a fuller experience of the same life in the age to come. The age designated in the Bible as *the age to come* is not heaven; it is the establishment of the Messianic Kingdom upon this earth until all the covenants, which are described as eternal or everlasting in the Scriptures, and promises of God have been fulfilled. It should be obvious to all the reasons that the God described in the Bible cannot leave such covenants and promises unfulfilled.

Acts 10-11 is an extraordinarily key passage for correcting the message that Christians have preached for over five hundred years. Not only does it not provide NAR any support for its belief that faith in Jesus is the only way a person can be forgiven and get to heaven, it actually contradicts that belief altogether.

Cornelius was *already accepted* by God *before* he heard about Jesus.

He was already righteous without being given Christ's righteousness to make him so (remember: the belief that Christ's righteousness must be given to a person before he can stand before the throne of God's judgment hoping for acquittal comes from a theological perspective being forced upon the Scriptures, rather than an exposition of the Scriptures).

Furthermore, since there was no mention of any need to take care of his sins, we have to suppose, based upon the authority of the Scriptures themselves,[1] that such a need did not exist or is irrelevant to the point being made. Cornelius needed to hear about Jesus and learn all the things that He had taught His disciples[2] while He ministered among them. But none of these new revelations would offer him a free ride to heaven or get him any closer to heaven than he was already.

Jesus preached *the gospel of an earthly kingdom.*[3] He did not preach *the gospel of grace* formulated by Christendom. Anyone who fears God and does what is right is acceptable to God. You ought to believe that because it is the clear statement of the Scriptures.

---

[1] 2Tim. 3:16-17 assure us that we have all that we need to adequately understand the Scriptures by what has been written for us in them.
[2] Matt. 28:19. Cf., also John 14:26.
[3] Matt. 4:23; 5:1 – 7:29; 9:35; 21:28-32; 24:13-14.

# Chapter 11

# The Teachings of the Apostle Paul
# On the Exclusivity of Christianity

NAR moves on to the apostle Paul to try to find in his writings support for its belief that only through faith in Jesus can heaven be attained. When asked the question "Do you believe that a Jewish person who sincerely practices his religion without accepting Christ is going to hell?" The author of NAR answered with a very blunt, "Yes."[1] He then amplified his response in this way:

> "… you can't *go to heaven* without faith in Jesus Christ as your *Savior.*"[2] (emphases mine)

Remember that in NAR's formulation of the doctrine of soteriology, salvation is having a Savior rescue you from hell so you can go to heaven. That is the reason I emphasized "go to heaven" and "Savior" in NAR's statement. If you have read NAR, you have not seen a single verse employed there that *explicitly* says what NAR believes to be true in the quote above. The urgent question for you, the reader, then is, "Why do you believe what NAR is saying?"

When it begins to quote the apostle Paul, it is interesting that it doesn't allow some of Paul's inspired words to carry much meaning. The reason? They would contradict its entire premise. For example, when it quotes Phil. 3:6 in which Paul says that *as far as the righteousness required by the Law goes, he was blameless,*

---

[1] NAR, p. 121.
[2] Ibid, p. 122.

NAR doesn't expound upon those words at all. That statement by Paul is a show-stopper. But it does not seem to faze the author of NAR in the slightest. I suspect that he has been trained, like I had been, to *suppose* some inadequacy in Saul's spiritual condition before he became the apostle Paul. Consequently, Paul's righteousness was *somehow* deficient from that demanded by God. It was *somehow* inferior to what he was *supposedly* given by God the moment he trusted in Jesus (According to NAR's teaching on justification, Paul was given Christ's own righteousness the moment he trusted in Jesus.).

The religious training that is expressed in NAR has kept the author from understanding the relevance of Paul's statement. Paul is basically saying that *he was already in a right relationship with God, living righteously as God had commanded him to do even before he came to faith in Jesus.*[1] Paul's revelation of this truth relative to his own life is not simply his opinion or his self-evaluation. It is given under the direction and inspiration of the Holy Spirit.[2] The religious training of the author of NAR has prevented him from seeing and receiving the truth of Scripture. It happens. It was true of me for over thirty-five years.

What, then, is Paul saying? He is saying that he had no need of being *given* Christ's righteousness when he believed in Jesus because he was *already blamelessly righteous* by following the Law of God in faith. This, of course, is a very important truth to assimilate in order to correct our sub-culture's present theological grid. *If Paul did not need to be given Christ's righteousness in order to be righteous before God, is it possible that others today don't need it either? Is it possible that no one actually needs it?* Needless to say, such a

---

[1] That fact, of course, has ramifications in understanding both the character of God and the *supposed* total depravity of man.
[2] Relate 2Tim. 3:16-17 to 2Pet. 1:20-21 and 2Pet. 3:14-16.

concept as this would make all of NAR's arguments null and void. This understanding of Paul's point in Phil. 3:6 would overturn the present understanding of justification.[1] In fact, it would declare the current view of justification to be unbiblical, unneeded, and even destructive. Paul was already in a right relationship with God before he began to trust in Jesus (whether that is called salvation or justification, it does not matter). Others in the NT were as well.

As NAR continues, it asks this poignant question,

"If everyone is going to heaven *regardless of his beliefs* or if there are multiple routes that lead to the same destination of heaven, then *why did Paul endure all the suffering* (including his own death) *to preach the message of Jesus Christ?*"[2] (emphases mine)

As I have already labored to explain, no one goes to heaven simply because he has believed in Jesus. Every final judgment of God described in the Bible is based upon works. *Belief is never the issue.* NAR has *assumed* that belief in Jesus is necessary to go to heaven because it has been taught a theological perspective that is built upon that conviction. As you should have noticed by now, NAR has yet to offer any valid proof for that conviction.

It won't do to manipulate the situation before us so that NAR's position can appear to work. That is done by saying that belief in Jesus is the requirement for going to heaven but once you get there, you are judged by your works (or at least by your *good* works as some would limit the judgment). Such circumlocution does not work for the simple reason that *belief in Jesus is never set forth as a condition for going to heaven.* There are those in the OT who went to heaven but who had, as far as God's sufficient

---

[1] This discussion is addressed in my book, *Acceptable to God without being Saved?*
[2] NAR, p. 124.

revelation is concerned, no faith in Jesus or in a coming Messiah. Even those who did believe in a coming Messiah, no text ever says that they did so in order to obtain a heavenly destiny or the forgiveness of their sins. *This teaching is sheer supposition based upon assumption after assumption.*

The truth is no one misses heaven because he hasn't believed in Jesus. Taking this idea a step further, we can say that good theology won't get you into heaven; bad theology (according to the Christian plumb line) won't keep you out of heaven. Believe it or not, the Bible is not about finding the right road that can get a person to heaven.

Hence, evangelism is not for the purpose of getting people to heaven. It should be for the purpose of explaining to people how they can live in a corrupt world and yet be holy, blameless, virtuous, wise, and spiritually strong as they reveal the character and will of the one true God. The *life* that Jesus offers will provide all that the trusting person needs to live this way. All that is communicable from Jesus to man is available for him to experience in *the life* that Jesus gives.

This isn't the first time that NAR questions the validity of evangelism if the purpose of evangelism doesn't involve making a person acceptable for heaven.[1] This misunderstanding of the central message of the Bible and how the real message ought to be, but isn't, the content for evangelism are as revealing as they are heart-breaking if I understand NAR's position correctly. In other words, it is saying that if there is no need to lay out for others the right path to heaven, then there is no need to go to them at all. NAR *assumes* that all men around the globe are consumed with the goal of getting to heaven when they die. I suggest that

---

[1] Cf., NAR, p. 121.

whatever desire for heaven we might find in people around the globe might be there because of the influence of Christianity's mistaken doctrine of exclusivity upon their culture. How unfortunate!

Our churches today are lethargic, dying, or dead because our members have become anesthetized, at least in part, by *the gospel message we preach*. Yet, each person has been given divinely appointed stewardships for which he must give an account when he comes before God's tribunal. Assured of heaven, many church members have become all too complacent upon earth. We ministers have produced this lethargy by the gospel message that we preach each Sunday. Then we incessantly rail against the lethargy, lukewarmness, and indifference that our message produced in the lives of the people allotted to us. When will we tire of this vicious cycle?

It only takes a quick review to conclude that the apostle Paul didn't contribute to NAR's defense of the doctrine of the universal need of all men to believe in Jesus to go to heaven. Rather NAR has to *assume* a great deal to make Paul a relevant contributor to its defense of this doctrine. If Jesus' claims don't lend support to NAR's defense, and if neither Peter's nor Paul's classic statements lend support to NAR's defense, what should we conclude? We ought to conclude that NAR's position is defenseless, Biblically speaking. We ought to conclude that its message is a distortion of the real message of the Bible.[1]

---

[1] Cf., Gal. 1:7.

# Chapter 12

# What about Those who Have Never Heard?

The more logical an error is the faster it is believed. The more logical an error is the less it will be questioned. *The orthodox, Christian teaching on soteriology is the unquestioned belief in the errors of man's past systematizing efforts to make the message of the Bible coherent and clear.* For over five hundred years, Christianity has taught that only by believing in Jesus can a person go to heaven. More and more people are being awakened to the apparent tragedy of this idea. That belief leaves the vast majority of individuals without any exposure to the one message that would give them an opportunity to go to heaven. Without that opportunity, they apparently are bound for hell by default. We must verify or reject the proposition that believing in Jesus is the only way a person can go to heaven. It can no longer remain an *assumption.*

NAR devotes a whole chapter to those who have never heard of Jesus. It realizes the anxiety that many of its readers have over its exclusivistic message concerning Jesus. Many today will balk at the idea that it is either belief in Jesus or hell for everyone. Consequently, NAR protests on behalf of its sensitive readers,[1] saying,

> "'It's not fair that God would condemn to an eternity in hell people who have never heard of Jesus Christ.' That severe punishment seems grossly unjust for people who, for whatever reason, have never been exposed to *the good news of Christ's willingness to*

---

[1] NAR, p. 133.

*forgive those who trust in Him for salvation.*" (emphasis mine)

The protest is a good one. A Biblical answer needs to be given to it. Notice carefully the highlighted words in NAR's statement. *Does the good news, the gospel, include Jesus' willingness to forgive those who trust in Him for salvation?* Do verses spring into your mind that *explicitly* set forth that proposition? Shouldn't you wonder why they don't?

NAR supposes that an answer to this seemingly harsh, even cruel divine judgment upon those who have never heard of Jesus can be supported by considering four principles which it thinks the Bible teaches. Those principles are as follows:

1. Everyone is guilty before God.
2. No one is saved apart from faith in Jesus Christ.
3. Everyone has received a knowledge of God.
4. Anyone who wants further knowledge of Christ will receive it.

That is exactly what I was taught, and what I taught for over thirty-five years. In addition, that is also the message of virtually all the evangelical seminaries and Bible colleges throughout America. How can they all be of one mind and yet that mind-set be errant? The answer is simple. Satan is real, and he has our ear. His goal is to deceive us and lead us astray. He is excelling at his goal.

But for our purposes, let's investigate these four principles to see if they are true and, at the same time, capable of relieving the harsh portrayal of God that Christianity's exclusive gospel creates. My goal is to give the reader a big picture perspective on these principles and their ramifications. A more detailed picture will have to wait for a better time to be drawn.

In my opinion, the exclusive gospel that NAR presents characterizes God as a tyrant who creates all men, assigns each creature his area of habitation, and then judges each one based upon whether he had believed a message about Jesus which may not have been given to him. According to NAR that is what orthodox Christianity teaches. This isn't a message that a thoughtful world is likely to continue to receive much longer without much better proof that it is correct. Christianity has greatly benefited from not beginning its evangelistic approach to those of other religions with such a message. But it is becoming harder and harder to hide these beliefs, or at least to down play them, from the intelligent seeker.

## Everyone is Guilty before God

Another way that NAR says everyone is guilty before God is to say that *hell is everyone's default destiny.*[1] This is NAR's representation of orthodox Christianity's belief. Unless each person is saved from his default destiny, he will certainly end up in hell. NAR insists that it is incumbent upon each one to understand the bad news so that he can better understand and receive the good news. The bad news, according to NAR is this:

"we are all guilty before God because of sin."[2]

Even if this proposition is accepted as true, why should we *assume* that the sentence or judgment for each and every sin is hell? Let's agree that we are all guilty before God because of our sins. But why should we conclude that the penalty for our guilt is an eternity in hell? Are there verses that *explicitly* tell us that the penalty of *any* sin is an eternity in hell?

---

[1] NAR, pp. 109-131. This is basically the point of chapter six.
[2] Ibid, p. 135.

That doesn't sound like a just God, much less like a loving God. There is no revelation that assigns hell as the inescapable penalty for a personal sin. That Christianity has made that connection is based upon *conjectures* and *assumptions* alone.

After a little more reflection, doesn't the penalty of spending an eternity in hell seem a bit extreme?

A white lie gets the same penalty as murder?

Stealing food to keep from dying of starvation gets the same penalty as mass genocide?

Being angry with a person gets the same penalty as murdering the person?

Lusting after a person gets the same penalty as committing adultery or rape?

I think deep down everyone knows that there ought to be different penalties for different sins. Deep down everyone knows that God would not act in the way that NAR has *assumed* He must act. If parents intuitively know that not every disobedience from their children merits the same discipline, doesn't it naturally follow that God would have different penalties for different sins?

Is it true, or is it just another *assumption,* that God holds each person accountable for every sin he commits? Jesus seems to teach from the cross that some sins of ignorance will not be held against some people. In fact, He asks the Father to unilaterally forgive those sins because they are *sins of ignorance.*[1] We should remember also that the apostle Paul had basically the same view of things as Jesus expressed on the cross.[2] And if God can treat one person this way in one instance, aren't we required to conclude that such a treatment of people must not be against His character? Aren't we entitled to assume that He may treat others that way

---

[1] Lk. 23:34.

[2] 1Tim. 1:13-15.

too since He is immutable and can't change?

It is important to understand that NAR is setting forth the traditional, orthodox position for a large part of Christendom. According to it, there is no alternative: believe in Jesus or go to hell. I am not questioning whether a person is guilty before God because of his sin; I'm questioning the idea that every sin, or any sin, justly merits an eternity in hell. If this is true, why doesn't the Bible tell us that clearly and *explicitly*?

## No one is Saved Apart from Faith in Jesus Christ.

NAR's first point, that everyone is guilty before God, naturally flows into its second point. If man is guilty before God, and hell is the penalty for his guilt, then he needs to be saved from that *supposedly* eternal punishment. NAR never proves the most important part of its first point: that an eternity in hell is the penalty for each and every sin a person commits. This foundational premise is just *assumed* to be true. As a result, we are naturally led to question the veracity of its second point: that salvation is obtained only through faith in Jesus Christ. But first some clarity is needed. As in the case of the first point, NAR *assumes* the truthfulness of this point. In addition, even the meaning of the term salvation is left unproven.

For NAR, being saved is being saved from hell and given a free gift of heaven in hell's place. Since Jesus never offered to be any "believer's" Savior from hell, it is futile to defend a proposition that was never made in the first place. NAR *assumes* what ought to be proven.

If salvation isn't a deliverance from hell accompanied by a gift of heaven, then what is it? Is it possible that salvation could be so radically different from the concept that the author of NAR and I have been taught, that it is incorrect to say that belief in Jesus is the only way a person can be "saved?" That is the case.

Take for example the salvation of Matt. 1:21. Jesus was supposed to come in order to save His people from their sins, right? First, we need to determine what the Bible means when it speaks of a salvation *from sins*. When Jesus came upon the scene for ministry, what was His message?

His message was not about His death for sins though He did die for the sins of the whole world.[1] His message was to believe that He was God's Messiah in order to have eternal life,[2] an abundant life,[3] a supernatural quality of life[4] that is nothing less than the actual life of Jesus[5] flowing through a person as he trusts Jesus for it.[6] Since Jesus was sinless, His life flowing through a person could make that person sinless as well. While that is the potential of a person who is trusting in Jesus, whenever he ceases to trust in Jesus to provide His life, the flow of Jesus' life ceases to produce his adequacy for all things. Jesus was offering Himself to be a Savior from sins in a way that no one had ever experienced before. To be saved from sin by Jesus was to be made a "super-conqueror" over every sin man was asked to deal with.

But it is a fact that in every nation under the sun men have overcome sin apart from the life that Jesus offered when He finally stepped onto the pages of history. Take Job,[7] Abimelech,[8] and Joseph[9] as three examples when almost every patriarch of the

---

[1] John 1:29; 1 Cor. 15:3-5; Col. 2:13-14.
[2] John 6:47.
[3] John 10:10b.
[4] Rom. 8:35-37.
[5] Eph. 3:16-17.
[6] Gal. 2:20.
[7] Job. 1:8.
[8] Gen. 20:5-6.
[9] Gen. 39:7-9.

OT could be used as well. The point is that people in every age have been saved from sin without trusting in Jesus Christ for that salvation.

We also know that believing in Jesus could save a person from his own corrupt generation.[1] But Daniel was saved from his without ever trusting in Jesus.[2] Others have qualified themselves to be saved into the kingdom that is coming[3] without believing in and following Jesus or a promised Messiah.[4]

Consequently, once again we must conclude that people, without believing in Jesus or in a coming Messiah, have been saved from the exact things that Jesus came to save His people from. Depending upon whether the terms salvation and saved are understood Biblically or not, it is clear that people have been and will continue to be saved from their sins as they trust in God, even without believing in Jesus.[5] Others by loving God and loving his neighbor as he loves himself will be saved into the coming kingdom of Messiah[6] without believing in Jesus or in a coming Messiah. Consequently, we have no real reason, other than it happens to be the official position of our sub-culture's orthodoxy, to say that only by faith in Jesus can a person be *saved*.

An objection may be raised due to the fact that these salvations are not spiritual salvations from hell. Because they aren't, some would argue that salvation by Jesus alone has not been disproven. The answer to this objection is simple. The only kind of salvation that Jesus offered was one dealing with this present life. He never offered to save a person from hell.

---

[1] Acts. 2:40-47.
[2] Dan. 1:3-16.
[3] Cf., Matt. 8:11-12.
[4] Lk 10:25-28.
[5] 1Cor. 10:13.
[6] Lk. 10:25-28.

There are, of course, two salvations that only Jesus can and will accomplish. There is the salvation of the person who has believed in Jesus from the coming Great Tribulation.[1] This salvation, apparently, is not dependent upon a present, vital faith in Jesus since the good and the wicked are all taken up together.

The second salvation that only Jesus can accomplish is the deliverance of the faithful and righteous into His kingdom upon His return to earth.[2] This salvation will require a vital faith during the years leading up to the kingdom's establishment.

It should be immediate clear that neither of these two salvations are the ones that NAR is focusing upon. The only salvation that it is discussing is the supposed salvation from hell to heaven.

## Everyone has Received a Knowledge of God

NAR's third principle builds upon the first two. NAR moves from the guilt of all men who necessarily need a Savior to the fact that everyone has some revelation from God that convicts him of his guilt and need of a Savior. This revelation goes out to all men leaving them without excuse for not seeking God through the Savior that He has provided. The problem is, according to NAR, that there is no such thing as a "sincere truth seeker."[3] Such an idea is simply *fictitious*, it says.[4]

Where does that leave us? According to NAR, we have a person who is guilty of hell and who, in his present state, can't do anything about it. While God's revelation is supposedly convicting him of his guilt and of his need of a Savior, nevertheless, he has no capacity to seek God or to come to God for a solution to

---

[1] 1Thess. 4:13—5:11.
[2] Mk. 10:23-26.
[3] NAR, p. 148.
[4] Ibid.

his sin and guilt. In other words, while God has provided a Savior, that Savior is of no use to the guilty party because the guilty can't actually seek the Savior for the salvation that He is offering.

As I understand it, although man can comprehend his dilemma and his need because of God's convicting work upon him, yet he is not able to comprehend or come to faith in God or in God's provision for his need. One has to wonder how such a scenario renders mankind without excuse or why God would ever trouble Himself in the first place to communicate to man if he can't respond to His communication in a positive manner and if He didn't plan to do anything else to help him. Surely an omniscient God would know better. Surely a solution that can't be utilized can't be a valid foundation for man's inexcusability. That leads us to NAR's fourth principle.

## Anyone who Wants Further Knowledge Will Get it

Since sinful man can't come to God on his own, how does he come to the point of *wanting* further knowledge of God? This is the place where God's election unto salvation comes in, according to NAR.[1] This doctrine is foundational for all Calvinists. God chooses those who will come to Him to be saved because, *supposedly*, they can't come on their own. With that divine elective choice, God also gives grace to open the heart and motivate the chosen one to come for salvation.

The reader is given the last puzzle piece that gives NAR's answer to the question, "What about those who have never heard of Jesus?" How is it fair or just to send those people to hell when they have never heard the only message that could keep them out of hell? The answer in short is they are already condemned by just

---

[1] NAR, pp. 151-54.

being born into the world. They are already guilty and the penalty for their guilt is an eternity in hell. Why are they guilty? Because, somehow, they participated in the sin of Adam and Eve and thus were condemned along with their first parents. Consequently, when they are born into the world, they are born with that guilt upon them.

But, don't you see, this begs the question related to the death that Adam and Eve incurred with their first sin. What does that death refer to? Why is it *eternal* (which is not a possible interpretation because the Hebrew term for eternal is not even used here, and, if it had been, is not synonymous to the English term eternal)? And why is this death related to hell (supposedly)? Our current theological understanding has no Biblical basis for the answers that it gives to all of these questions.

If you think like a theologian, being guilty for a sin that you did not consciously commit may make perfect sense. But if you think like a normal man on the street, it makes little sense at all. On the one hand, those who have never heard of Jesus are not going to hell because they have never heard of Jesus; they are going to hell because they were born into this world guilty of having already sinned against God before they were born. Hence, *God is supposedly just for sending those to hell who have never heard about Jesus because they were already going to hell anyway.* Such reasoning may get a pass from some, but for others it will never be acceptable because it destroys the clear teaching of the Scriptures that God loves the whole world and not just a select group chosen out of the world. The typical verses used to argue for this innate culpability of man can be easily interpreted in other ways.

According to God Himself, real love meets the needs of the one being loved as God Himself requires in 1John 3:16-18. That requires God to solve the problem that the people He is loving have. If He did that, and we are required to assume that He did, man's supposed total depravity has been solved (assuming he had such a thing to begin with), leaving him free to respond to God's overtures as he wishes.

In conclusion then, the first principle fails because it has no Biblical support that *explicitly* affirms that man's guilt before God is worthy of a sentence to hell for the rest of his existence.

The second principle fails because there are instances in both testaments describing individuals being *saved* without believing in Jesus. And they are saved in exactly the same way that Jesus was supposed to save people Himself. Thus, Biblical *salvation* did occur apart from faith in Jesus. This is not denying the fact that there are some salvations that can only come through Jesus as I delineated earlier. It only denies that Jesus saves a person from hell through a single, one-time response of faith in Him.

The third principle is true: all men do have a knowledge of God. But that principle is incorrect when its content is about needing or wanting heaven and an escape from hell. Making that the content of the knowledge is pure conjecture.

The fourth principle is also true as far as it coincides with the Bible's message about this present life and God's desire to walk with all men even more closely than ever. But once again, the increased knowledge is not about what is needed to get to heaven, but rather what is needed to walk in righteousness with the God of all creation.

When all of these objections are added up, the conclusion is obvious: God would be unjust to require faith in Jesus from those who have never heard about the need to have faith in Jesus in order to go to heaven. Fortunately, the message of the Bible is not at all about finding a road to heaven.

Which is worse: never hearing about Jesus or having been taught a misleading message about Him? As I search the Scriptures, I have to conclude that it is the latter rather than the former that is the worse condition to be in. Since believing in Jesus will not get a person to heaven, and since the unconditional benefits of the cross of Jesus accrue to all men apart from faith in Him, the best situation to be in is the one that only requires two things from each person for him to be acceptable to God today and, thereby, to be assured that he has nothing to fear at his own personal judgment. According to the clear statement of Scripture, *if a man fears God and does what it right, he is acceptable to God now.* That acceptance will not be overturned in the day of judgment because God can't condemn later what He accepts or justifies today.

Join with me to pray for a revival. It appears that only by such an intervention of God will the Christian faith awaken to its real state of affairs. May God forgive us all for being a part of the propagation of such spiritually numbing beliefs as we have sown in the hearts of God's people for over five hundred years.

* 9 7 8 1 9 5 0 0 7 2 0 2 6 *